Ollie's Kids

Calvin H. Bowers

Published by: DocMo Enterprises

2136 West 82nd Street

Los Angeles, California 90047

 (323) 816-7635

DocMoEnterprises@gmail.com

Distributed by: Professional Publishing House

1425 W. Manchester Ave. Ste. B

Los Angeles, Calif. 90047

323-750-3592

www.Professionalpublishinghouse.com

Cover design: Damon Saddler Design, Carson, CA

First printing February 2012

978-0-9714661-0-4

10987654321

DEDICATION

This book is dedicated to the memory of my mother, Ollie Mae Ella Ray-Bowers and to all the women like her who worked with little as they sought to rear their children in the context of hard work and spiritual principles. May this book also inspire all mothers to raise their children in the love and admonition of the Lord and never give up on them. And finally to my eight siblings, five who did not live to see this book. They all loved me unconditionally and helped shape my life to become Calvin Harrison "Doc" Bowers.

ACKNOWLEDGMENTS

No work is an independent effort; therefore I am indebted to many who helped to bring this book to its completion.

My sibling's filled out questionnaires, shared pictures and stories that made up much of the content of the book. My three children Crystal, B., and Lori all had a hand in the development of this book beginning right after the release of my first book *"Realizing the California Dream,"* in 2001. My son B. did the typesetting and also served as an editor in every phase of the writing. Crystal, my oldest daughter made many helpful suggestions. She served as my project manager, keeping us on a timeline and worked as a liaison with the publisher. My baby girl, Lori who is always in my head was a good sounding board and gave her input as we progressed with the writing.

The three secretaries at the Figueroa Church of Christ Pamela Thompson, LaShon Thompson, and Vernell Robinson all assisted in doing whatever they were called on to do, especially with my scheduling which allowed me the flexibility to write more. My faithful wife Barbara Ann showed great understanding and patience in my efforts. She helped to schedule my time so that my interruptions were minimized as I wrote. Enough cannot be said about my graphic designer Damon Saddler. He worked many hours beyond his regular job by formatting photos and creating the cover for the book. He is a brilliant Christian young man and I am very thankful to have him and his wife Angelique in my family circle.

A special acknowledgment goes to my publisher and now friend, Dr. Rosie Milligan, who guided the work from start to finish in a kind and professional manner.

Finally, I accept full responsibility for all errors made or misinformation that may have been included. I am eternally grateful and above all blessed by all who were and still are a part of my family quilt and life journey.

With respect,
Calvin H. Bowers

TABLE OF CONTENTS

ABOUT THE AUTHOR

Bowers has lived in Selmer, Tennessee; Decatur, Illinois; Terrell, Texas, and Los Angeles, California. He is professor emeritus at Pepperdine University, after having served on the faculty and administrative staff for over 35 years. He earned a doctorate degree in higher education from the University of Southern California. For 46 years, he was the chairman of the board for the National Youth Conferences for Churches of Christ. He has served as the minister of the Church of Christ at 57th and Figueroa for over 50 years.

Bowers was married to the late Mozell G. Bowers for 46 years, until her sudden death in September, 2004. Calvin and Mozell have three children: Crystal Deneen Bowers-Guy (daughter, Taylor Elaine Guy—nine years old), Byron Calvin Bowers, and Lori Desta Bowers-Bailey (daughters, Madison Mozell Bailey— five years old and Regan Ella Bailey—two years old). In 2006, he married Barbara Hayes from Clinton, Oklahoma; she encourages and assists him in his work.

Bowers resides in Los Angeles, California, where he continues to travel the country, lecturing, conducting teaching and leadership workshops. One of his ultimate goals is to extend the ministry of Fellow Workers for Christ to train 1,000 ministers, teachers and leaders.

FOREWORD

Calvin Bowers is a man of wisdom and a man of God. It is clear that his family, his upbringing, and his background formed the man he is today. The strong, powerful, African American family structure that has always served to nurture a people through struggles and hard times is the cornerstone of this powerful memoir. Calvin Bowers is the man he is today because of his family, his personal strength, and his faith in God.

Families who read this book together can find hope as well as humor, suggestions as well as inspiration. If we can save the family, we can save the future for the next generation and those to come. Calvin Bowers has given us a guiding light so the path of faith and family can be illuminated for all.

I consider Calvin Bowers to be my mentor and friend. I've known him for many, many years, and he's always offered a calm, wise solution to any storm that crossed my path. It is an honor to introduce this book to the world.

Dr. Sharon M. Draper
Author and Educator
Graduate of Pepperdine University
1997 National Teacher of the Year

Introduction

Working at the Clock—It's Time to Go

I ARRIVED IN THIS WORLD APRIL 8, 1932, born in the midst of the Great Depression. This is the story of my family and our journey. From my grandparents, to my father and mother, to my brothers and sisters, to me, your guide on this journey, to my children, and to my grandchildren. A journey out of the Depression, out of a Jim Crow south, and across this great county. I was born eighth of nine children, born to Henry and Ollie Bowers of Selmer, in Tennessee. Of those born before me were Sarah Vernell and William Verdell, Verble Mae, Major Ross, Rose Mary, Dorothy Magdalene, and Herbert Hoover.

Selmer was a sleepy little town in West Tennessee, where highways 64 and 45 came together with 64 continuing eastward toward Savannah and the Tennessee River area and 45 continuing southward toward Corinth, Mississippi. In many ways, it was an average southern small town of that era.

After I graduated from McNairy County High School in 1951, like most of my brothers and sister had before me, I had no idea what I was going to do. So I found myself in the downtown unemployment office. As I recall, it was nice and cool with an electric fan softly dispersing the air. While waiting to be called, I thought to myself, this would be a nice place to work. In that moment, as my mind drifted off into dreams about coming to work in a place like this, living at home with my parents, maybe getting my own car, and working with the local churches in Selmer, the voice of the secretary brought me back to reality.

"Calvin Bowers," she called out, as though the office was full of people. Actually I was the only person. "You may go in now." Her voice showed no hint of warmth nor gave any implication that you might feel favored in any way. It seemed more to question: *"What are you doing here?"* and *"Ok, let's get it over with."*

As I entered the door to the small office, I saw a middle-aged white man who sat behind the desk, who got paler as I drew closer, and who was slightly overweight. As I look back, he could have benefited from the job he was about to offer me.

"So you want to go to work?" he asked.

I thought, *why do you think I'm here?* But I answered in my most professional voice, "I sure do."

"Mr. Smith needs some help out at the Clock Truck Stop. Go out there and tell him I sent you."

The morning sun was beaming hotter as I walked the half-mile from the office, to the Clock Truck Stop, where Highway

45 and 64 merged on the outskirts of Selmer. The owner had an almost boyish look about him and it was clear to me, as he spoke, that he was not a southerner. In curt language, he told me what the job was about, asked me if I wanted it and when I could start.

As he told me about the other employees and what he paid each, my heart and my hopes began to sink. "I pay my highest man, Tackett, $37 a week, and I can pay you $23 per week."

Not much money, I thought, but more than enough for me to accept.

As I walked the two miles back home, I reconciled myself to pumping gas, washing cars, and the other odd jobs around the truck stop. Was I in for a surprise? I had hardly noticed the highway crews breaking up the concrete, part of plans to open a whole new business area in front of the truck stop. My last worry was that helping to do this was a part of my assignment. Arriving at work the next day, I was introduced to the wheelbarrow, expected to push it, full of concrete, to where the front area was being poured.

Seeing that the concrete was swaying from side to side and that the wheelbarrow was going to turn over any second, the foreman of the project came to me and showed me how to grip the handles with my fingers and to lean forward, using my weight to move it. This helped some, but as the sun grew hotter, the wheelbarrow got heavier. After going to the water fountain several times, the foreman remarked out loud, "I can't keep that boy away from the fountain."

Thank God for Lenny Lusk, though. As lunchtime grew near, it occurred to me that I had no lunch, nor did I know where I could go to buy something. This older black man, who was working with the company, was the father of some of my friends in school. His sons, Lenny Jr., Chuck and Peter, were close to the ages of my brothers and me. When the foreman said, "Lunchtime," Lenny came straight to me and said, "Come and go with me." Little did I realize that I was about to have an experience I would never forget.

Although Selmer was very segregated and I had lived there all of my life, I had avoided going in backdoors and to "colored" windows because I had basically lived among other blacks and ate at home. But that day was going to be different.

Dripping with perspiration, Lenny and I walked the half-mile back into town to a white café that I had seen often. I followed Lenny as he went straight to the backdoor of the kitchen, stopping just inside the door with his hat in his hand.

"What can I do for you today, Lenny?" the cook asked, clearly indicating that she knew him well, while all the time eyeing me. Lenny flashed a big smile and said, "I'll have a hamburger and a bottle of Coke." "I'll have the same," I added.

The next step of this episode was something I will never forget. I experienced something that was an everyday occurrence to Lenny, but was almost disgusting to me. "Follow me," Lenny said, still smiling as the cook handed him our burgers and took the money. The frosty bottle of Coke felt good to my tired hands and the warm feeling of the hamburger, with the smell of fresh cut onion, made me realize how hungry I really was. I was anxious to stop and see just where, and how soon, we could stop and eat. Out the door, around the corner and back on the main street, Lenny went, with me right behind him. To my surprise, we came to the front of a lawyer's office, which was on the second floor. As Lenny entered, ahead of me, he turned and said, "The lawyer's not in today." So I followed him halfway up the dimly lit, narrow and creaking stairs and when he stopped, I stopped, and there we ate our hamburgers and drank our Cokes.

I do not even remember enjoying my food. I was overcome with a flood of mixed emotions that almost made me sick to my stomach. Looking back, I can better sort out these feelings. Just out of high school, I was among the very top students. Thoroughly segregated, the teachers had taught us that we were as good as anyone. As a student minister, I had even been selected to deliver the baccalaureate address and had received more awards than anyone else in my class. I recognized that we had paid just as much for our food as those folks sitting comfortably in the front, so why did we have to sneak out and climb halfway up those stairs to eat in fear of being caught by the lawyer, who could have just decided to drop by his office on his day off? All of my being shouted out that this was not right, but I never said a word about it to Lenny. In fact, looking back, I say thank you to Lenny for reaching out to me and showing me how you had to live every day, and lighting a fire in me, so that I would join the future fight to keep others from having to live that way.

All of this happened in the one hour given for lunch, walking all the way back to the Clock, I hardly said anything. In fact, I do not recall the rest of that day. I supposed the energy from anger fueled me for the hard work ahead, because I completed the day without incident.

When I received my first paycheck of $23, I gave $3 to my mother to help out around the house, where it was obviously needed. I managed to save most of the rest.

To my surprise, the manager called me a few weeks later to inform me that he was moving me to the night shift. I was to begin work at 6 p.m., and would work till 6 a.m. five days per week, with no increase in pay. The work was somewhat easier; at least it was cooler. However, a different type of work was added: pumping gas, changing oil, changing truck tires, and washing trucks. Changing tires on cars is relatively easy, but you try changing the tire of an eighteen-wheeler, when you weigh less soaking wet and holding a brick, than the tire. These tires were so huge that you could hardly tell that the air was out of them, once you removed them from the truck.

This kind of challenge soon began to make me think of creative ways for improving my situation. One day, while cleaning the gas pumps, which were another one of my duties to keep me busy, I concluded that there must be a better way. Then I thought about going up north, where my older sister lived, in Decatur, Illinois. She was a kind person with a kind husband who would be willing to help me. I thought of this as I worked for the next few days, and this idea kept returning to me.

Then it happened. I had spoken several times at the Oak Grove Church of Christ in Henderson, Tennessee. The people there seemed to like me. I received word from Luther Burgess, one of the leaders, asking if I could conduct the funeral service for Fletcher Howard. Although I had never delivered a eulogy, I agreed to do so. However, this meant getting off work at 6 a.m., going twenty miles away to conduct this service, and returning to work by 6 p.m.

That day the supervisor met me and pointed to a huge truck that needed to be washed that night. I do not recall how many times I almost went to sleep trying to wash that truck. Looking back, I am surprised that I had not fallen off the big stepladder and hurt myself.

In the morning, the truck actually looked worse than when I had started. It was not finished, but I was. There were so many streaks on that truck that it didn't look like it had been washed at all. I said to myself, "Okay…, but this is it. I am quitting and going up north. Time has run out at the Clock." I quit that day.

❄ SECTION 1 ❄
They Keep Coming

Chapter 1

Ollie Mae Ella Ray

MAJOR RAY WAS A STRONG DISCIPLINARIAN who frequently raised his voice at his family. He took pride, however, in Ollie Mae, his only daughter, and he was so pleased because she turned out to be a beautiful girl and a good worker.

It was a hot day and Major Ray had given strict orders to his only daughter, Ollie, to meet him with his lunch at noon by "The Big Rock." This well-known landmark was a place family members had met at many times. Ollie knew the place well, having played often in that area.

Knowing how easily her husband could get upset when his orders were not carried out, his wife Sarah made sure that the lunch was prepared on time and that Ollie was well on her way. Arriving at the Big Rock a bit early, Ollie was a bit surprised when her father was nowhere to be seen. She waited and waited, but there was no sign of her father. Finally, her only recourse was to retrace her steps back to the house.

Nearing the house, she saw her father and knew right away that he was extremely angry. Without a word, he began whipping her with the mules' plow lines. For what, she didn't know. The tears that began to fall were from pain as much as confusion. She had done what he had told her to do. In the midst of the pain, she noticed her hand was bleeding.

Her father never gave her a chance to explain herself, as deep as the pain became. Nor did he ever explain what she'd done to upset him. He never apologized. She never forgot.

Maybe that was the reason she never forgave him. Maybe that was the reason she later ran away from home to marry Henry Bowers, our father. Maybe her mother had identified this incident as "just another" of Major's frequent flare-ups. Whatever the long-term impact, Ollie made it clear that all of her nine children knew of this incident and that her father wronged her.

She always ended the story with, "I made up my mind that I would never punish one of my children without giving them a chance to explain what they were accused of doing." This, among many other reasons, was why she was so special and we, and others, loved her so much.

The lesson here is to never neglect to discipline your children, but realize that they have rights too and do not let the discipline become a violation of those rights. Such actions could end up making the child bitter.

Knowing her as Ollie Bowers, my mother, I had to wonder where did she get her drive, how her thinking developed, and how did she learn her approach to life? She was able to complete an eighth grade education and apparently liked school. She also had a desire to attend the Southern Bible Institute in Mississippi. There is no indication that she received any type of encouragement from her parents for this desire, so it had to come from other aspects of her environment.

Her uncle, Dave Crowder, was an educator, and was obviously a big influence in her educational passion. Somehow, he managed to receive a college education from a school in Nashville becoming one of the few black veterinarians in the state of Tennessee at that time. He later founded a high school, and a street was also named after him. His school remained opened for years after his death in 1944.

Dave married Anna Bell Holt, a member of the prominent Holt family, on Christmas day of 1900. This family consisted of landowners who held as much as three hundred acres in the Hooker's Bend area, where Ollie lived. The family also included a number of educators, both men and women. Many of the men in the family were in the military during World War I. They had their own community, Holtsville, where they later developed a school, had a store and even a community cemetery. They were also known as a kind and benevolent family who helped many who were less fortunate.

Following World War II the family members began migrating to northern cities, such as Chicago, Detroit, Cleveland, and Dayton.

When I visited Detroit in the 1980s, there was a church elder there named Granville Holt. In a casual conversation, I asked him where he was brought up. He replied, "From a little place you probably never heard of. Hooker's Bend, Tennessee." When I told him that my mother was from that area, he replied, "I remember Ollie Mae. She was a pretty girl." We had a good laugh, and I concluded, "I am going to have to tell my dad about this."

This was just another indication of how close Ollie was to the Holt family, and she was obviously influenced by their successes. As a child growing up, my mother made frequent references to Uncle Dave and the Holt family.

I heard her often say Freddie Holt was her best friend growing up. From an ancestral study of one of the Holt's descendants, I learned that Freddie Holt was the youngest daughter of John W. and Mary Garrett Holt, who owned a general store and served as postmaster in Holtsville, Tennessee.

Freddie is described as being extremely close to her father. She was fondly remembered riding her horse, "Dolly," alongside her father to meet steamboats on the Tennessee River. From there they delivered the community's mail. Freddie attended the exclusive Bradley Academy in Murfreesboro, Tennessee, which began to serve African Americans in 1884. She passed away in 2004 at 104 years of age.

There are possibly a number of ways that Freddie, as a best friend, could have influenced Ollie. As a horse rider, she could have influenced Mom's "tom boy" ways, which were also encouraged by her mom's brothers. From her family's background, she most likely had a great impact on her thirst for education, which was to become a lifetime vision for Ollie, for herself and her children.

Henry Harrison Bowers

Henry Harrison Bowers was born October 29, 1891 and died October 8, 1986. He was the second child born to Martha Jane and William Verdell Bowers. Other children born to this couple were Sherman, the oldest, usually called "Giant," Arthur, the third son following Henry, and the two girls, Zelphia and Jessie.

In those days there seemed to be a trend of marrying what was known as "up," color wise. On my father's side, my grandfather Verdell, who was very dark, married my grandmother, who was very light. I later learned that Verdell's mother was a Creek Indian and "black as a pot," according to my dad. On the other hand, my grandfather described his dad, "Lem" Bowers, as half-white, with hair that curled up from underneath his cap. In my dad Henry's case, he and Uncle Arthur were very light-skinned and Sherman and the girls were darker. He often described himself as a "red nigger," who was born with two teeth.

Henry was a small man, no more than five feet and six or seven inches in stature. He was a quiet man who minded his own business and knew how to stay out of trouble. I remember him as a gentle man, who never severely punished his children. He usually made them mind and punished when he had to, but frankly, I don't remember him giving me more than one whipping.

Due to the work to be done on his family's farm, Dad's education ended at the sixth grade. He did learn how to read and write, which was more than many of his day. In spite of limited opportunities, he became quality carpenter, self-taught, who knew how to also paint, lay brick, build shelves, swings, and do most work in the field. Plumbing and electrical work were before his time, but I am sure that he could have taught himself those skills as well. I often wondered how far he would have gone, if he had been given more opportunities.

He worked for blacks and whites. Mrs. Nina Mae Latta, whose husband owned the Latta Ford Motor Company, and whose land we worked, sharecropping, used Dad frequently for work at their house. She was always pleased with his work and his price too, I suppose. Many times they worked close to our school, and students would tease me about my dad sitting in the back seat of her car on the way to a job. I knew exactly why, but I would play it off by asking, "How many black men do you know have a white woman as their chauffer?" Then we would all laugh because we knew the reality.

I often wondered why Dad seemed so angry so much of the time when I was coming up. As I grew up, I understood that was what he had to do for our survival.

"Some days," he often said, during the Depression, "I would go to town and stand around all day just to make a quarter." On Saturdays he would stay at the grocery store until closing time to get a bargain on fruit, which would have spoiled before Monday. The owner would say, "Henry, I will let you have all of the leftover bananas for fifty cents," or, "These apples have rotten spots and you can have them for thirty-five cents." We were always waiting at home to enjoy whatever he brought.

Due to his kind nature, he always brought something special for my mother: a piece of bologna, crackers, and a Pepsi soda. Sometimes he would bring some cheese. Mom would share whatever he brought with those of us that were still awake.

The Wedding

Rumor had it that Ollie had left her clothes at Uncle Dave's house with the expectation of the day and time that Henry would arrive.

This time, instead of coming the thirty miles by mule, he hired a white man to drive his car to Hookers Bend to pick up Ollie.

I recall Dad telling me that after they picked her up, he could imagine her father coming out of the bushes at on mule back at every turn. When the car blew out a tire, he just knew that it was Major Ray shooting at him. On their way, after fixing the tire, it was not too long before they arrived at the house of Henry's parents in Selmer.

There was a big crowd of family and friends waiting for them. The preacher was there and ready. Everyone had to look the bride over and make his or her comments. Evidently, Ollie passed their inspections with high marks. The ceremony was short and the celebration began, lasting well into the night. Their new legacy was to begin on that day.

From every indication, the first months of Ollie and Henry's marriage were happy ones. They had their own private room with a comfortable bed at the home of Henry's parents. Martha, Henry's mom, did all she could to make the young couple happy. She sensed that Ollie must have missed her own mom and Dad and the rest of her family, so she encouraged Ollie to talk to her about anything she felt a need to talk about. After all, having two daughters of nearly the same age helped her to understand Ollie's concerns and need.

Zelphia and Jessie, Henry's sisters, had much to talk about because they too were approaching marriage age. They talked and giggled as they worked in the fields together, always admiring this pretty young girl whom their brother had married. Since Martha did not have to go to the field to work, Ollie was happy to go in her place because she liked the field better than the housework.

To her surprise, Ollie noticed that she was beginning to experience morning sickness and frequently an upset stomach. By this time, she and Henry had moved to Falcon, a little community about a mile from Henry's parents, if you went the short way. The talk of the possible pregnancy became more of an obvious reality as weeks passed.

On April 12th, it became obvious that it was time to call Dr. John Smith. Dad remembered that he parked his car right alongside the road. During this time, it was a common thing to use midwives and some had suggested that to Dad, but he would have none of it. Ollie never experienced pain like she did during the delivery. Her joy when it was over was short lived when the doctors said; "There's another in there." To her surprise, the second was not nearly so painful. The first was a girl, to be named Sarah Vernell, after Ollie's mother Sarah. The second was a boy, to be given the name William Verdell, after Henry's dad.

Word of the twins spread quickly over the community. Friends and neighbors came from far and near to see the Bowers' twins. Ollie and Henry were happy, but her heart was longing to see her mother and father. The arrival of the twins only increased this desire.

The day did come for her to return to Hookers Bend. She had the personal joy to go to her mom and dad carrying a baby in each arm. Her arms were tired from carrying them but joy overflowed between her and her family. Their anger at her leaving had turned to joy. All was forgiven and forgotten at the sight of these children.

Having twins brought great joy and gave Henry and Ollie a feeling of being special, but it raised a number of questions.

Financially, it was going to be tough taking care of one new family member, but two was unexpected and unimagined. This meant two of everything. Ollie also had little experience taking care of babies and taking care of two was going to test her limited skills. Even two girls or two boys would have been easier. Had they been the same gender, they could have worn each other's clothes and shared other things as well, but a boy and girl was an added challenge.

Ollie never complained, but her work was harder. Henry never complained, but I do remember him telling me that sometimes sitting before the fireplace in the evenings, one of the twins would slip out of his lap and fall to the floor. He would pick it up by its gown and put it back into place. Fortunately, neither of them was ever seriously hurt.

As they began to grow it became obvious that Vernell, the older, was also the leader. I remember Mom saying that she never crawled, but merely scooted along. I am sure it was so she could keep an eye on her younger brother. William Verdell, whom we always called Bill, did not seem to mind the attention.

Bill learned to read by looking at the newspapers used to paper the walls of our house. He showed signs of early intelligence, but initially, Vernell was in charge. Being the lighter complexion of the two, certain family members were more admiring of Vernell, but Bill got his share of attention because he was a male child and the second grandchild of the Bowers family. It was not long before he began to assert himself by chatting constantly with everyone.

When he was old enough to go to the local store alone, many times Mom would become worried because he would be gone for such a long time. It was at that time that he would be conversing with the older white men who would be sitting around in the store. He never spoke of any mistreatment or racial abuse; instead, they seemed impressed by this little black kid being so articulate.

In the meantime, Vernell became more relaxed about rivaling Bill, and turning her interest into other directions. It was obvious from the beginning that Vernell was going to be a caregiver. A trait she nurtured and extended all of her life. Not only was she the ideal "big sister," but also she cared for many. Somewhat like Harriet Tubman, she was responsible for so many family and non-family members leaving the South, including me in 1951.

Ollie found her to be very helpful with the other children in her early years. This probably is what prompted her to say of her later in life, "She never sassed me and was my easiest child to raise." Upon entering grammar school, teachers noted Bill and Vernell's intelligence and gladly promoted them with their grade level. Compared to other kids the twins' manners and home training were evident.

Bill continued speaking up for himself and talking himself out of fights with bullies. He never seemed to be ashamed by how poor our family was. He wore an old hat, which showed a ring above and below the outer band, made by perspiration. One day Willie D., a darker-skinned girl who had extremely short hair, way before it was fashionable, said to him, "I will give you a dollar if you get that hat cleaned." Without missing a beat, he replied with a devilish grin that would make the Devil himself blush, "I will give you five dollars if you do something about that hair." From that moment forward, she left him alone.

Bill and Vernell finished Selmer's Rosenwald Elementary School, which was equivalent to our middle school today. Where did they go from here? Was it back to the fields? Try to get a job with only menial type jobs available? End up in someone's kitchen as a housekeeper? With the influence of Uncle Dave, a principal in the Decaturville High School, and along with Ollie's passion for education, she was not about to let this happen.

The Twins go to High School

At the time after the twins' graduation from junior high, there was no high school for blacks in Selmer. With the exceptions of our second oldest sister, Verble, the rest of the children were later able to go to the McNairy County High School when it opened.

Uncle Ernest, Mom's brother, and his wife Mamie still lived in Hookers Bend. A bus ran by their house to the all-black Dunbar High School in Savannah. I am sure Mom hooked up the deal to send Vernell to stay with Ernest and Mamie, so that Vernell could attend high school. I do not know if Dad protested, but if he did, he lost. So off Vernell went, to Hookers Bend.

With Bill, it was not as simple. He could not stay with Uncle Ernest and the family had no relations in other nearby towns where he could be sent. I must admit that I draw a blank at this; I really do not know how he ended up at Lexington High School about forty miles northeast of Selmer. I believe they called this school Montgomery High.

I do know that it had a famous principal named Mr. Bonds, who came from a well-known family from around the Brownsville area. Some of those Bonds migrated to Memphis, Tennessee; Decatur, Illinois; and other places, and a number of them were ministers and teachers. I later knew a Robert Bonds, a minister in Memphis, and Lucious Bonds, a high school agriculture teacher who was my teacher at McNairy County High in the late 40s. I also knew a Roy Bonds of Brownsville. All of them that I knew were associated with the Church of Christ.

Bill spoke of Mr. Bonds, the principal, with great respect. He obviously was a strict disciplinarian who ran a tight ship. While Bill was in Lexington, we knew little about his activities. We do know that he lived in a boarding house with other students and worked for a while at Kroger Super Market. He told how they would give him grapes and bananas at the end of the week. We also knew that he graduated and had pictures of his graduation.

He always came home with stories to tell. I remember the story of when he received one dollar from home and how excited he was about that. This was not much, but it showed that there was still love for him from his parents and he appreciated whatever they gave him.

Looking back at both Vernell and Bill going away to school at about fifteen or sixteen years of age reminds us how difficult this must have been for them. Yet, both of them made it with very limited support from home. When I think of this, I feel that we owe Bill and Vernell a debt of gratitude for setting an example for the rest of us that followed.

Vernell Excels at Dunbar High School

Although we knew little about Bill's high school activity, we knew a great deal about the activities of Vernell.

She made more trips home when school was out to tell us about the school year. She played on the basketball team, acted in plays, did well with her grades, and had many friends, and later, a boyfriend. She told us how challenging the basketball practices were. She enjoyed her classes and her friends. The boyfriend, O.T. Parsons, was the love of her life, according to her at the time, and her favorite topic of conversation. In fact when Lena, one of our cousins, had her second baby, Vernell talked her into naming him O.T.

While in high school, Vernell taught a Bible class at a local church. After graduating, it was time to move on, but to where?

Verble Mae

When the twins were about two years old, Ollie realized that she was expecting again. It was not what she was anticipating, but she really did not object to it either. As challenging as the twins were, she looked forward to another child and watched as the days and weeks went by.

On June 17, 1920, another little girl was born into the Bowers family. She was a beautiful brown little girl with exceptionally bright eyes. She loved to smile and this made others smile back at her. They named her Verble Mae, after a white lady known to the family. Actually, she looked more like a twin to Bill than Vernell did.

About that time, Vernell was being called "Ick." I am not sure how she acquired this nickname, but I think it was after someone called her "Ichobod." The name stuck and soon all the family members were calling her "Ick."

Verble enjoyed following her sister around and trying to do what she did. Bill had lots of patience with her and tried to take care of her the best he could. Verble also had a strong attachment to Bill. He liked to play with her and nicknamed her "Kokomo." He encouraged her to be adventuresome. This got her in trouble with Mom a few times. He would say, whenever there was a task to be done, "Kokomo can do it."

Two things became apparent about Verble: she was an exceptionally bright student and she did not have the easygoing spirit of Vernell. In school, the teacher, Miss Little, recognized her intelligence and boosted her to advance in class. Verble enjoyed this and tried harder to please the teachers. If she were born today, she would no doubt be in an accelerated school program, but there was no way of testing to actually know her I.Q. Our parents had no way of knowing how smart she really was. She always spoke clearly, with confidence.

She had a kind, friendly demeanor and always smiled. She was easy to like. Behind that smile was the determination of a rattlesnake, though, and the readiness of the same creature to strike if not respected. One of my other sisters told of an occasion that a certain young man, D. Moore Wade, was harassing her. Verble stepped in to defend her younger sister, and slapped the boy so hard that he probably saw stars. He never bothered anyone in our family again. In Verble's later years, a much younger woman challenged her about something, ending her diatribe by saying, "If you were not so old I would not let you get away with this." Verble shot back, probably with her usual smile, "Don't let that stop you." I could hardly imagine a woman of her age, at that time, making a reply like this, but the younger woman left her alone. She was not known as a bully or a fighter, but she never let others walk all over her.

Being a very bright child, our great-uncle Dave Crowder, the principal of a high school in Decaturville, recognized her intelligence, offered to take her and send her to school. But Mom and Dad refused, stating that, "We do not have any children to give away."

I understood their reasoning of not wanting to give one child an advantage over another, and they did not want to run the risk to the exposure of immorality. Mom always warned my sisters that she did not want them returning with a baby in their arms before marriage. Although she did let the Vernell stay with our uncle Ernest to attend Dunbar High School, Great-Uncle Dave was not her brother, and she refused to make a similar opportunity available to Verble.

I have often thought how great Verble could have been with a good education. She thought clearly and spoke clearly and was often mistaken for a person with a much higher level of education.

Ollie and Her Quilting

Some of my fondest memories of my mother were being under a quilt-in-progress while she was quilting. I had a special sense of security with the quilt over my head and being near her.

I do not know where she learned this art, but she was good at it. First from many designs and patterns, she chose the quilt she wanted to make. Then she engaged in cutting and piecing. From old clothes of children, women and men she got her pieces. With that design for the quilt she would get squares or other shapes on paper and pin it on the back of the cloth, which allowed her to reproduce the design on cloth. When enough of these were made she would start piecing them together to eventually make a spreadsheet. The many colors from old shirts, blouses, pants or other fabrics were a beautiful sight to see.

Taking a plain sheet she would lay it on the floor and spread the patchwork evenly over it. Putting the designed spread over the top she would stitch the cover to the layer of cotton on the bottom sheet.

When it was ready to be put on the frame and tightened up the quilting process could begin.

Carefully, she would follow the designs with her stitches. It was like a cloud formation coming together forming a clear design or a butterfly coming out of a cocoon gradually evolving from a caterpillar. You saw it taking shape.

After several days of intense work she would say, "It is finished." All that was needed after that was to take it down from the frame and hem it. I never ceased to marvel about the process, and I will never forget it. Many winter nights I would wake up and thank God for the warmth of being under one or more of her quilts.

There were also many lessons learned from this process of quilting. First, she used what she had to get what she needed. Secondly, she had a vision of how all of these pieces would look together and how differences could add strength and beauty of the whole. Color did not matter but only made it more attractive. Finally, she showed that one has to stay with the task until it is finished to really enjoy it. Though she has been gone over thirty years, we still have some of the quilts and bedspreads she made.

She not only dreamt about the possibility of illustrating unity in the simple task of quilting, but she did something about it. Seeing how she created unity from diversity reminded me of the words of Jesus' prayer. He said: "I pray that they all may be one, as thou Father art in me and I in thee, that they also may be one in us: that the world may believe that thou hast sent me," John 17:20.

As mentioned earlier, Dad was an unusual carpenter. He proved that when he made a quality frame for Mom. He took two pieces of 1-by-2 lumber and drilled several holes at both ends. Then he took forty-penny nails to put them through the frame so that once the bedspread was attached to the backside of the sheet by rolling it up on the pieces and adjusting its tightness by putting the nails in the holes. Then it was easy for Mom to begin her quilting.

$$\mathscr{C}hapter\ 2$$

Dad's Religious Life

WE ALWAYS HEARD THAT DAD WAS a member of the Roach Chapel Methodist Church, but we never saw him go there. But there were clear indications that he feared God and was deeply religious.

He showed his fear of God by the storm shelters that he built and his fear of storms. He built these storm shelters by first digging a large hole in the side of a hill about six or seven minutes from the house. Then, he would cover the top with logs, placing tin over them and covering the tin with a mound of dirt. An entrance was made, a door was added and benches were placed around the walls.

This was literally a cool place, but I hated it. Sometimes canned fruit was stored there and many times there were snakes there when we went into it. This did not seem to matter when Dad got ready to go to the storm shelter.

When a storm was coming up Dad perched at the window to carefully watch it. Sometimes he would say, "It's going around," but most of the time he would say, "Ollie get the kids up we are going to the storm house." I did not want to believe my ears when I heard that. It meant getting up, half asleep and grabbing an old overcoat and heading out the door, sometimes in the rain, to the shelter. You could expect frogs and sometimes snakes to be there already. The only light was one lantern which Dad had leading the way.

Once the lightening, thunder and rain slacked or stopped Dad slightly opened the door and announced to the rest of us, "It's gone over or around now; we can go back to the house." What a relief we all had then. On some occasions the storm would turn around and we would repeat the process all over again. Throughout the process Dad would warn us to be quiet because, "The Lord's work is going on."

I often thought, "Isn't the sunshine the Lord's work too," but I never got up the nerve to say it. I knew Dad feared God.

The next religious clue he gave was his blessing, asked before every meal. I remember the blessing, "Gracious Father smile upon us. Make us truly thankful for the food we are about to receive. Amen." We heard this every time we ate and only he was allowed to say it.

The clue I most appreciated from him came at the end of the day. Every night he would get on his knees and pray to God. We never knew what he said and that was okay. But what a powerful example he left of loyal consistency. I will always remember him for that.

Church wise, he just could not buy "Julie's church." Unfortunately for him that was where his wife and the rest of the children all went. In the first place, he thought Julie, a heavy, dark-skinned woman with a loud voice, talked too much, especially to him. She would say things like, "When are you going to get in the church? We have all your family and we might as well have you." All the time he would be saying to himself, "Never. NEVER!" In the meantime, while he had this debate going on with Miss Julie, Ollie was leading all the children to being baptized into the Church of Christ.

I was the middle child of the last three children, and when I saw Herbert go up, give his hand to Brother Hannah the evangelist from Corinth, Mississippi, I followed right behind him. In fact, there were two sets of brothers baptized in that meeting: H.B. and Maxwell, the Smith brothers, in addition to the Bowers boys. We all were baptized about three days later in Hartman's Creek in July of 1947 when I was age fourteen.

When we arrived home that night, I do not know who told Dad but he became very angry and grabbed a quilt and went outside for rest of the night. My mom never said a word. Everything seemed well until I gave my first brief sermon about ten days later. He confronted me and said, "Cal, you are not trying to preach are you?" I really do not know what I said, but I have thought many things I could have said since that time. Years later after Miss Julie had died and all of us children had left home, he was baptized in the Church of Christ and remained faithful until his death.

Returning home one summer and speaking for my home church in Selmer, he called me to the car where he was sitting after church that evening and said, "Boy, I am sure glad that you became a preacher." I had finally received that blessing. As years rolled by, I realize more and more what a great man Henry Harrison Bowers was and I am proud to be his son and to bear his middle name.

The man never complained although walking many times two miles with a twenty-four pound sack of flour on his shoulder to feed his family.

The man carried a hammer, a saw, and a square in a bag on his shoulder or his back to earn a living for his family. To me, he will always be a great man and a worthy example. My mother made a great pick worth waiting for.

The Arrival and Early Years of Major Ross

A little over two years after the birth of Verble, the second baby boy was born on December 20, 1922. He was a light skinned baby with curly hair, which was destined to change in a few years. Based on what our mother told us, a number of people asked for a lock of his curly hair; Major often bragged about his "good hair" when he was a baby. We teased, and told him that they should have kept a lock for evidence. Major was always curious about how things.

He tried to follow in the footsteps of his brother, Bill, but early on their relationship was not always the best. It is a theory that the second boy born into a family seems to have a tougher time, maybe due being overshadowed by the first.

Often Bill seemed to put him down, calling him "Midget" and criticizing his efforts when he failed. But Major fought back, making up in effort what might have lacked in strength and skills. From a very early age, he was a hard worker, as if he had something to prove. He worked harder in the field, picking cotton, sawing wood, and he became a mentor for his younger brothers, Herbert and me.

He played games, such as baseball, with neighborhood boys James "Son Baby" Bowers (a cousin of ours), Mose Harvel, Charles Lockert, and his brother Z.T. Amos. They were all great friends and did many things together. Major became very clever and enjoyed playing tricks on others. I knew well because Herbert and I were the victims of many of his pranks. When Bill came home on a visit he called Major's bike a piece of junk. This was not surprising because by this time we had grown and were used to Bill's putdowns, and maybe he did it just to make us all try harder.

I do not really believe that Major ever liked school. Maybe it was because his two younger sisters were in the same grade with him as freshmen in high school. Anyway, he quit school at the tenth grade and went to work. It was also strange that about this time, he got his own car.

Rose Mary

Rose Mary was born March 2, 1925 in Falcon, Tennessee, where my parents first lived after moving out of Henry's parents' house. Falcon was just another small nearby community in the vicinity where Henry had lived all of his life.

Rose Mary was born on Monday morning at about 8 a.m. before the doctor arrived. Mrs. Gertrude Smith, a friend of Mom's, put on the baby's first clothes. She was a pink little baby with curly hair. A white lady suggested the name Rose Mary after a friend of hers; Mom liked the name and it stuck. Shortly after her birth, the family moved closer to the rural area of Selmer nearer to Henry's parents. His parents sold him a parcel of land and he built a house where all of the rest of the children were born. Rose Mary took her first steps in the new home.

As the fifth child, Rose Mary had the four older children to protect her and would eventually have the four younger siblings to care for. "Rosie," as we came to call her, enjoyed and filled that role quite well by her easygoing ways and her willingness to work hard.

Rosie recounted several incidents from her early childhood to me before her passing on: "Once, when I was about three years old I was hungry and asked Mom for some food. She told me to get it from the stove. A hen was in the house and after I had gotten my bread, she jumped in the stove and began pecking the bread. I was excited and slammed the stove door and cut the hen's head off. As she was bleeding, flopping and dying, I was scared. I ran and got my red coat and headed for Grandmother's house. When Mom missed me, she ran and caught me; although she did not whip me, I got a stern lecture that I never forgot. I imagine that hen ended up in the pot for dinner."

She recalled an incident when Dad left his buggy parked in front of the house. "I picked up the part of the lines which were the lightest part and the mule moved and ran the buggy over me. This knocked me out causing much excitement. Thoughtfully, Mom poured water on my face and brought me back to life."

She also recalled a third incident: "Once we were working in the field called 'The Mulberry Tree Patch.' There was an older boy named Rassie Ray, who lived in one of Grandfather's houses in the town of Selmer. He was the grandson of Hattie Short, a friend of Grandfather's, and he was sent to help us work in the field. He didn't know how to work so he 'picked' at me all day, until I got tired of him and told Verble. She said, 'Do something about it.' I picked up a rock and hit him upside the head. Blood streamed down his face. He left me alone after that. When I arrived home and told my mother she said, 'I must hear both sides of the story.' When he passed our house, Mom asked him, and he admitted the truth. She did not whip me, but she gave me a good lecture."

She also remembered the many games our mother taught us and how of our parents taught us how to work.

As one of the younger children, I remember Rosie as my big sister. She was a hard working, caring person who got along well with others. In fact, this may have caused some problems because not only did she not participate when others did wrong, but she would tell our parents.

She took it upon herself to help both younger siblings and other children who walked back and forth two miles from school each day. She recalled, "Before we went to school each day, I had chores to do, and then watch for the little ones on the way. The cars were swift and the roads were muddy; however, I guess I was the one who had to do it. Fortunately, no one ever got hit or hurt."

As her youngest brother, she would often come and straighten my shirt, fix my collar or even tie my shoe at school. She would come and see about us whenever anything went wrong. I do not ever recall her having to fight for us. She was also a good worker in the field and could pick more cotton than most of the children. While they were playing, she was working and often picked as much as two hundred pounds in a day.

As my sisters Rosie and Dorothy got older, boys started paying attention to them. As they talked of boys going to and from school, they developed their own code so we would not know what went on. We never knew whom "I" actually meant, or whom "you" actually meant. So when they would say, "So *you* came up and said this," or "Then *I* got in the conversation," we did not have a clue as to what they were talking about. The only way we ever broke the code was to watch with whom they talked to at school. We never let them know that the code was broken.

Rosie was introduced to religion and the church earlier in life by Mom. Mom taught all of us about the will of God and how important it was to do it. She introduced us to scriptures like, "God so loved the world that he gave his only begotten son, that whosoever believed in him should not perish but have everlasting life," John 3:16, and "Not everyone that saith unto me Lord, Lord shall enter into the kingdom of heaven; but he that doeth the will of my Father which is in heaven," Matthew 7:21. She would go on to share the story of the two builders that built houses, one on the rock, and the other on the sand. They both were tested by the rains, floods, and the winds. The one on the rock stood and the one on the sand fell, according to Matthew 7:24-27. Later she would emphasize this point to me concluding by saying, "Calvin you are laying a foundation for a man." I never forgot that.

She also emphasized later on the importance of being baptized for the remission of sins as the people did on the first day of Pentecost after the resurrection of Jesus. Just as Peter told the people when they asked, she also taught us, "Repent and be baptized every one of you in the name of Jesus Christ for the remission of sins and ye shall receive the gift of the Holy Ghost," Acts 2:38. She also taught us to follow the example of David when he said, "Thy word have I hid in mine heart that I might not sin against thee," Psalms 119:11.

Rosie reflected on her early religious teaching, "Times were hard and money was scarce but our hard work and our love for God carried us through. Our mother taught our first knowledge of God. My first Sunday school class was in the house where our older brother, who was good in his books, became our Sunday school teacher. Uncle Maude Lusk and several neighborhood children came to our house," she said.

I introduced the point of religion in connection with Rosie because her religious teaching had such a profound impact on her life. She later became the wife of a struggling preacher, James Dixson, and helped him to become an excellent biblical scholar and preacher. Together, they inspired me as a teenage preacher to seriously study the Bible and to continue my education.

Dorothy Magdalene

Dorothy Magdalene was born in Selmer, Tennessee on January 18, 1927. She was the sixth child born into our family, and one of the brightest. Although she and Rosie were closer in age than any of the others except the twins, they were different in many ways.

I often thought of them as two pieces of the same puzzle. Just as puzzle pieces are different when they are joined together they make each other stronger in a complimentary way. If all pieces of the puzzle were smooth and alike they could be put together but would have added much to each other. However, with the projections of one piece perfectly fitting with the indentions of the others, strength and cohesiveness is added.

This was the case when Rosie and Dorothy; they were inseparable in school. Just as Dorothy felt challenged to follow Rosie around, she was also motivated to try harder. This type of effort landed her in the freshmen class with two older siblings, Major and Rosie.

Rosie was the sweet, quiet, innocent looking girl who would not hurt a fly. Dorothy was the outgoing girl who would ask you a question, then ask you another if your answer failed to satisfy her.

Rosie would obey without questioning. If our parents told her to keep the younger kids, that was fine. If they told her to go to the field to work that was fine too. She was mainly an indoor person.

On the other hand, Dorothy was an outdoors person. She preferred working in the field to cooking or doing any housework. She liked wandering through the woods, exploring flowers, listening to the birds, and communing with nature.

She loved humor and had a great imagination about how the rest of her siblings would be when they were older. I had no doubt that she loved me as her little brother; but she sure made it tough on me in her imaginary world. She pictured how my future would be as a preacher. It was not pretty. I would have a wife and house full of children. While I would be up preaching in some little backwoods church, my wife would be trying to take care of the kids. Part of the time I would be trying to preach with a baby in my arms. I began to think that either she did not think much of my future as a preacher, or she was preparing me for future difficulties that I would face.

Ollie Loved Fishing

My mother loved fishing and she linked up with many different partners who went with her to the creek bank. As her constant companion, I was with her through the whole process of the fishing trips. These trips were always taken after certain jobs were done. She had to fix the food, hoe the garden, wash the dishes, clean the house, and take a break to talk to cousin "Pet" or some other friend who happened to drop by.

Her plans for this trip were always laid out a day ahead of time. First, we had to dig the earthworms, which was always my job. I knew the best places to find them. The moist earth beside the hog pen, or near where the mules stayed in the stables always provided a good supply.

In fact, I became quite good at digging up earthworms. Mr. Pole Estes, a white man who liked to fish, paid us twenty-five cents per hundred worms we provided. I actually dug enough worms to buy a cheap suit with short pants. So when Mom assigned me to dig, she had her man. The supply had to be ample because we dare not to run out of bait when the fish were biting.

As the bright sun came up on our little town and movement stirred she arose with fishing on her mind. All morning chores had to be done quickly before we set out to the creek on Mr. Hartman's farm. Sometimes we would go to the small pond that was also on his farm.

Either place we went, the results were always predictable: a few perch fish, a few catfish and occasionally a larger fish that was nearly a foot long.

Another function that I did was to go ahead on the bushy and seldom followed path looking at hanging branches and clearing the sides of the path so that there were no snakes present. Finally reaching a spot where we thought they would be biting, again I had to make sure there were no snakes around.

As a young girl, a snake had bitten my grandmother. Even though it was non-poisonous, it gave her the fear of a lifetime that was passed on to Ollie and eventually to us. One evening, just after dark, Sarah was standing close to a bush when she heard a noise that frightened her, so she quickly moved away.

"On second thought," she said to herself, "that was probably nothing," and she bravely moved back close to the bush. Right at that point, a snake quickly sprang from the bush and struck, leaving her frightened with the thought she might be dying. This left her with a lifetime fear of snakes.

Ollie was afraid of snakes, so she always took her a snake killer along with her. Guess who that was? Me (of course).

She had her own procedure for how to kill a snake. First, be aware of hissing or sliding sounds, slithering through the grass or leaves, and be absolutely quiet until you discovered the snake's location. It may have stopped or intended to change directions, but you had to kill it if you could.

Before leaving home for the creek bank be sure that you had a hoe or a good sound stick that would not break. Quietly, get as close to the snake as possible and swing to get one good lick, preferably on the snake's head, then the follow through with another as quick as possible.

She often told us after you hit him the first time, you must "mend your lick." This concept has been with me for life, and it expanded to other areas of my life. It has come to mean that in whatever situation, after you make your first impacting contact, you should rapidly make another, without allowing time for recovery by the desired object. After many times applying this principle, I can witness that it works.

I also remember the simple fishing equipment, beginning with two long cane poles, which often grew near the water's edge. Lightweight twine would then be tightly secured to the pole in two places, so it would not slip off. A hole was then made in a cork, usually from a snuff bottle, to slide the string through so that it floated on top of the water, in order to tell when you were getting a bite. She always reminded me, "When he takes that cork under give a strong yank to hook him." After arranging the cork a piece of lead was attached a few inches from the end of the string for a sinker and the actual hook was tightly secured at the very end of the string. Put on a live, wiggly worm and you were ready to fish.

I never actually knew if the fish could hear us or see us, but if you interrupted mom when she was getting a bite, expect to get a backhanded smack to the side of your face.

I will never forget the joy she had when that cork started bobbing and the even greater joy when it went under water. A quick snatch landed the small fish over her shoulder and left it wiggling on the ground. She would often give a glad cry, "I got him! String him up Calvin, and bait my hook again." I knew the drill: take the fish off the hook, stitch a string through its gill, that string being tied to a stake stuck in the ground, and place the fish back into the water to keep it fresh for dinner later on. Doing this as quickly as possible, I would rush to bait her hook so that she could resume her fishing.

I often wondered how this process would have worked if she had caught a ten pound fish, or even a two pound one. Truthfully, that never happened.

Chapter 3

I Found a Nickel

MY GRANDMOTHER, MARTHA, COULD NOT READ nor count money. Granddad Verdell taught himself to read and count money. He was able to purchase sixty-five acres of land, more than any of his children ever dreamed of. In fact, he sold land to several of them, including my dad, as a place to build their houses on. I saw him as a clever old man who did not play too much.

He farmed his own land, rode a mule to town and occasionally had a little too much to drink. On those times he would ride by our house singing, *Amazing Grace*, or *A Charge to Keep I Have*.

One day, Martha found a dime, without knowing what it was worth. She took it to Verdell and with great excitement she said, "V.," as she called him, "I found a nickel." Chuckling as he took it he said, "Yeah. I found me a nickel too."

Ollie's Kids Growing Up

All of us were never at home at the same time, since Vernell and Bill had to leave Selmer to finish school before Jewell was born. However, most of us were together for different periods of time. This provided many humorous incidents and situations we will never forget.

Bill was very intelligent and also very clever. My dad built a small chest, with a lock and key, for several important things, including seeds for the next year's planting. We had consumed all of the peanuts that were set aside for eating and the rest locked away in the chest for planting in the spring.

Bill, the "clever one," figured out a way to get some of those peanuts without a key. He used screwdriver to remove the hinges. Entering from the back, he helped himself to the peanuts and screwed the hinges back on when he finished. He repeated this once too often and this was his undoing. Frequently removing the screws made the holes bigger and bigger. When Dad raised the lid to the chest it fell completely off. He knew something was wrong and quickly discovered that his supply of seed peanuts had been depleted. He had suspicions of whom the culprit was, but could not prove it. That criminal was never brought to justice.

Lesson learned about wrongdoing: when you get comfortable you get careless, then you get caught.

Herbert Hoover

December 19th of 1929, Henry and Ollie's third son was born. Running out of suitable names, they thought of giving him a name that might inspire him to be great, so they named him Herbert, after the President of the United States at that time. During that time, it was popular to name children after presidents, and especially, if you were black, Republican presidents. Unfortunately, as Herbert Hoover Bowers began to grow up, President Hoover's association with the Great Depression made him very unpopular and left little room for bragging that one was named after the president. In fact, I never heard him brag about it.

I remember my mother saying that Herbert was her most difficult birth. Other than that, Herbert arrived without fanfare. Word came down that he was a cute baby. He had plenty of playmates with six other brothers and sisters. Herbert also became one of Dad's favorite children among the boys. Several of the siblings have said Herbert was Dad's favorite son. Maybe that was because when he came along Dad felt a need to have someone with him to help out. I cannot say why for sure, but he was the one that followed Dad around the most. He remembers stories that I never heard of. However, there was no respect of person when it came to going to the field to work.

Over a period of time, Herbert would acquire a number of nicknames. Bill would call him "Big Zollie." Guess who got called "Little Zollie?" If you guessed me, you are correct. In school, he was called "Bantum Rooster" by his friends. Grandmother always said he was like "Jack Redding," and Dad referred to him as "Hub".

From as far back as I can remember, Herbert was always a major influence in my life. To begin with, he was left-handed and so was I. I often wondered if my left-handedness was natural or influenced by him.

Looking back, I would say that he was an adventuresome kid, always trying new things. I will never forget my first day at school. I remember being left in the classroom by Herbert and running to him when school let out. Within a few days, the newness wore off and I joined in the fun.

As we grew older, there were always chores waiting for us when we arrived home from school. First, it was out of the school clothes and into the play or work clothes. We had to carry water from the spring under the hill. Next, we had to cut the wood for the fireplace as well as the cooking stove. The measurements were twelve inches for the cooking stove and twenty-four inches for the fireplace. Sometimes we sawed the wood with a crosscut saw or chopped it with an axe. Then, it had to be neatly stacked on the front porch.

After doing homework, we took turns with our other siblings listening to our Sonora radio. We liked to listen to *The Lone Ranger*, Gene Autry, *Captain Midnite*, *The Shadow*, and *The Green Hornet*. When it was time for our parents to listen to the war news, we retired to the back room and read comic books. After a double check of the kitchen to see if there might be any leftovers, we headed for bed, because you knew you would have to get up early.

Usually our room was cold despite the heavy number of quilts on the bed. When Major, Herbert, and I slept in the same bed, we had to all turn over at the same time to keep the cover from falling off and to the floor.

Fortunately, getting up to start the fire in the morning was mostly done by Major and Herbert. I got into the act on the tail end. They learned to make this task into a special art. Beginning with sprigs of wood, they would move to chips of seasoned pieces of wood. When these pieces were burning larger pieces of green cut wood were added. They burned slowly and lasted longer.

Morning tasks before going to school, in addition to making the fire, included bringing in water, feeding the mules and milking the cow. It seemed that both Mom and Dad could always find something for us to do, even on Saturdays.

Dad cut our hair because we accepted the fact that was one of the things fathers were supposed to do. We definitely did not like the cut, but what could we do about it? Nothing. He would do what kids called a bowl cut, which looked like someone but an inverted bowl on your head and cut around it. When boys at school asked, "Who cut your hair?" I either knew what the next comment was or what they were thinking.

Speaking of Me

As children say, when ending counting in the game of hide-and-seek…"ready or not, here I come." On April 8, 1932 I arrived in this world. With the difficult birth of Herbert between three and four years before me, in the middle of the Great Depression, with seven kids already, I was added to the Bowers family. In an attempt to add inspiration by association, I was given a president's name too. Calvin was not too bad, but thank God it wasn't "Calvin Coolidge," which the kids in school promptly added anyway. I was glad that my parents went with "Harrison" instead. As I grew up I always felt that my dad's mom, Martha Bowers, influenced this. She was the only one that ever called me, and very persistently called me, "Harrison." I learned later that my dad Henry Harrison Bowers was named for President William Henry Harrison. I realized I was stuck with the names of two presidents. Maybe this was because somebody felt that I needed a double dose of inspiration. I later learned that neither of those presidents did very much. At any rate, as I reflect on this name, it always gives me a good laugh and a smile. We always remember positive things others said about us.

I remember Robeanus Westbrooks saying that I was the most beautiful baby she had ever seen. She never went further into explanation; maybe it was because she thought I needed to hear it, or that she had not seen too many babies, or that she'd had too much to drink when she told me that.

I cannot remember life without Herbert. The influence that he had on my life was conscious and unconscious. He influenced my every early action in life. Many of those influences remain with me today. Thank God he is still around.

When I began this writing, I sent questionnaires to all my siblings. One of the questions that included was, *what was I like as a child growing up*? They were kind, but frank. I asked this question to gain some insights about myself that I probably would have never recognized.

Their statements ranged from a me being a little boy who seemed to always have molasses on his bib overalls, to a kid sitting in his mom's lap when it was time to eat who always bumped his head on the table. One said if a brother borrowed money or anything else from me, I would pester them until they paid it back. My oldest sister said I was a cute little brown-skinned boy. Although my dad did not fill out a questionnaire, I remember him saying that I was as "stiff as a by george" and on another occasion saying that I was "vimmy." Since I did not know what *by george* nor *vimmy* meant, I concluded that "by george" meant not good and *vimmy* meant good. I let it go at that. Neither did I pursue further explanation of what my brothers and sisters said.

As far back as I remember, it was obvious that we were poor. We did not get many new clothes and I got my share of hand-me-downs. We got one pair of shoes for school in September that were supposed to last until the following April, and then went barefoot during the summer. Although we never went hungry, the word "leftovers" was rarely uttered. It was more like, "Are you going to eat that?" We could never afford to eat in the school lunch program although it only cost about fifteen cents per day. We would eat breakfast and do without food until we returned from school.

We appreciated folk who gave us things. Sometimes we would get a box of used clothing from Uncle Dave and Aunt Anna, Mrs. Mable Prather, or from one or two white families well known to our family. Once the box was opened it was a free-for-all trying to get an item that fit you. Sometimes nothing exactly fit anyone, but we always found a way to wear every piece.

Most importantly though, we never doubted that we were loved. At the end of the day, we all came home and ate a family meal together and talked about things of family interest. The following morning our assigned person got up and made the fire. Mom got up and cooked breakfast as Dad got ready to go to work, and as we got ready for school. Not eating was the sign that you were not ready for work or school. This was the culture into which I was born and had my first experiences of life.

It seemed that I was always well protected. I would see my brothers and sisters at recess and the teacher could send for them if they were needed. Mom's constant warning to the older ones was, "Take care of your baby brother and sister."

I began to see myself as a little brother with older siblings who would do things for me and who would in turn tell me what to do. I later learned in life that this was a dangerous position. Always expecting others to do for you expanded to your life outside of the home to school, the work area and life in general. I saw where it was necessary for me to begin making decisions for myself and accepting my responsibility for them.

In the home and in school, I learned to listen and follow orders, and maybe it was because I was half-scared to death most of the time. One day, when I was in the first grade, Miss Laurthree Westbrooks, our teacher, said, "Calvin, tomorrow you can read with the second graders." Overhearing that, two or three of the other first graders asked if they could read with the second graders too. She let all of us, including my first cousin Mary Ruth Lusk, move to the second grade. Most of us finished high school together.

Teachers also began giving me poems to learn, which I easily memorized. One of the first was *Three Little Kittens*. Another was *The Mirror of Life*, which ended with the line "give the world the best you have and the best will come back to you." I did not realize at the time that these poems were forming one of the foundations of my thinking for life.

One day I overheard two teachers say behind my back, "That Calvin Bowers is a smart little boy." That did wonders for my self-esteem. I had plenty of other negative influences later to give me balance and keep me from becoming conceited.

Although I may have possessed some native intelligence there were other influences of which they were not aware. Our school was not a one-room school, but there were several classes in the same room. If you were caught talking when other classes were in session you might get a warning or you could get a swift swat across you back with a switch. This was both painful and embarrassing. In addition, your siblings would report it to your parents.

As a second grader, when the first graders read, I listened for review. When the third graders had their classes, I listened for further preparation. This way, my learning was reinforced. Actually, I may have been more clever than smart.

In addition, I overheard my older siblings getting their lessons at home and this further enhanced my pre-learning for what to expect when I was promoted. Years later, I heard an education professor say, "The one room school was one of the greatest products of the early education system in the U.S.A." I may not go so far as to say that, but I agree that it had a unique quality.

In our fourth and fifth grade class, there was strong competition between the boys and the girls. I remember missing several classes due to illness. It so happened that during that time, they were covering fractions and long divisions. When I returned to class, Dewey Tuggle Jr. and Maxwell Smith took me aside, and soon I was caught up to the rest of the boys in the class and ahead of the girls. This was just a small example of the effectiveness of peer learning. I believe this is a method that still could be effectively used today.

When it was time for us to graduate to high school from the eighth grade, there was a countywide examination to determine the Valedictorian and the Salutatorian. I remember when our teacher received the results she said out loud, "You mean I got both of them?" Dewey Tuggle Jr. was Valedictorian, and I was Salutatorian. Although the teacher said it in appreciative way, in the tone of her voice I heard, *"I am going to have to prepare both students for their speeches."* I do not remember my speech at all, but I do remember a line from Dewey's speech. It referred to the gonging of a bell and as we were about to leave it seemed as if it were saying, "The last time, the last time!"

Dewey was my greatest competition in grade school, but how true was the bell that reminded us of it being the last time! Dewey was to go on to high school in Jackson and from there, to dental school at Maharry Medical School and later to the military as an officer and a dentist. I only learned what happened to him beyond the eighth grade in 2011 when I saw where he had made a donation to Southwestern Christian College. When I got his number and tracked him down he was living in Seattle, Washington experiencing some serious health problems. It was a joyful reunion to talk to him by phone, but as I am writing this, I received word that my friend passed away February 27, 2011.

And Finally, Ladies and Gentlemen, Introducing Jewell Irene

My youngest sister, and the last in the Bowers family, was born on March 20, 1946. They named her Jewell Irene. On that day, I distinctly remember my older sisters and brothers coming home from school and seeing the new baby. Little did I realize that my life was about to experience a drastic change. I have no recollection of the changing of my sleeping location, place at the dinner table or different treatments by my mom or family members, but from that time on, my little sister was always there.

I do not recall ever feeling threatened by her or intentionally or unintentionally letting her fall. She had light skin, sandy hair, and looked like the Gerber baby we saw in magazines. The older sisters, Rosie and Dorothy, adored her and she was the first child in the family to my knowledge to ever use a bottle. When they dressed her up and gave her that bottle, setting her in the middle of the bed, we all admired her.

Scientists argue about when life begins, but in another sense, I have no doubt when life began for me. I actually have no memories before Jewell was born, when I was almost four years old. Although Mom never used a midwife with any of us, she never went to the clinic or hospital either, so this birth must have been at the house too.

As she began to grow, she had a tendency to follow us around, and a tendency to tell on the older siblings. Our cousin, Son Baby, often came to our house. On one occasion when our parents were not home, Son Baby dropped a bowl and broke it. Although all the pieces were carefully swept up and disposed of so they would not be found, Jewell told on us in her jabbering way saying, "Son broke a bowl." We quickly ignored her, and the parents did not understand what she said. After a while, when one of our prized bowls came up missing, our mother put two and two together and reinterpreted what Jewell had said. To get to the truth, every one of us got whipped.

Since Herbert, Jewell, and I were too young to go to the field, Herbert and I had to keep the baby. We learned a great deal from each other and we lived with the strict word of our mother.

We soon learned that Jewell made a nice little servant to carry out our directions. We sent her on missions to bring us fruit and vegetables from the kitchen and even the garden as she got older. This ended when she wised up and brought in Mom as an ally.

It was not too long thereafter when we had a little hoe to chop cotton or a little sack to pick cotton. Our parents were clever in deploying their children as resources for work. As soon as they saw one's capability they put them to work whether it was picking up chips or milking the cow. It was not too long before Baby Jewell began to work too and she actually seemed to enjoy it.

No doubt about it, Jewell was mommy's baby. Mom called her the "poop girl" and she slept in the bed at Mom's back for several years. She followed her mother everywhere she could go. There never seemed to be any jealousy from the rest of us, but it did seem she got more than her share of bologna and crackers that Dad brought home to Mom on Saturday nights.

Being four years older, I was never in the same class with Jewell, but she probably followed the routine that some of us had earlier. She remembers having Bessie May Moore, who had been my teacher, as her first teacher. The first poem she learned was "Jack said I have a new hat and I have a new car, I am going to the place where the monkeys are." She also remembers walking two and a half miles to school with cold feet and frozen icicles sticking up out of the ground. Her older sisters had to carry her books and writing pad.

As she grew, teachers began to recognize her talents and to put her in skits and later plays. She was the only child in our family that ever took piano lessons. Her interest in music allowed her to be in the chorus where she also excelled.

Jewell remembers many things that she, Herbert and I did, like the time Major gave Vernell what he told her was a box of screws, and told her to put it up for him. Actually, it was a box of chocolate covered cherry candies, which he had bought for his girlfriend. She watched where Vernell hid it in a safe that had clothes folded up in it. When Vernell left, she came and told Herbert and me. We ate most of the candy and Vernell could not explain what happened when Major asked for his box. We did not tell, but Major always suspected that Dorothy ate his candy.

She also recalled the time that Vernell made suits for Herbert and me out of fertilizer sacks and dyed them different colors. After the suits had been worn for some time, Herbert discovered that one pant leg was longer than the other. After that discovery he refused to wear the suit.

Before one Christmas Eve, we found the stash of presents hidden by our parents. We took the cap guns, shot up the caps and put the guns back. All we got that Christmas was guns without caps, apples, oranges, candy, and nuts.

Our activities made me realize that kids left alone will get into many things. If the surrounding environment is negative, they can get into real trouble.

Jewell had a sweet disposition, cooperative with her teachers and was well liked by schoolmates. She and I were the last ones to be in school together. She also became a popular speaker, representing the school and in school plays. I recall one of her speeches, "I Am an American," winning a prize.

As I approached my last years in high school, we were the only two left at home. By then, the school bus ran right by our house full of other black students taking us all to the black high school. Several girls I liked, who also liked me, made their contact through Jewell, but those relationships soon faded after I graduated from high school.

In 1951, the year I graduated and left house, she remained at home with only Mom and Dad being there.

Now you see how we all got here and a bit how we began life. Not only did Ollie bring us into the world, she also did her best to lay a good foundation for each of us to build on. Our dad Henry did his part too.

We were very poor and knew our parents could not give us very much because they did not have it. They did give us a belief in the God of the Bible, and the basic principles: 1) Respect yourself and do not bring shame on your family; 2) Try to always be decent in the way you presented yourself; 3) Do not shame the family; 4) Do the best you can; 5) Put God first. This worked for us to the extent we followed it.

❋ SECTION 2 ❋
They Keep Growing

Chapter 4

Selmer

BORN IN THE MIDST OF THE Great Depression, I often teased Mom and audiences when I spoke of my family that I was glad that the pill didn't come along until the fifties. Otherwise, I might not have shown up at all. Mom said that Herbert, who preceded me by three-plus years, was her most difficult birth. When she learned that she was expecting another baby, this news was not met with a glad cry. After Herbert's birth, she often said, "I did not go to the barn lot for over a month."

Nevertheless, she never "played favorites." We all got whipped alike and she could always find us another job to do.

Blacks and whites rarely came together in Selmer, outside of workplaces. Even in these instances, the superiority of the whites was clearly pronounced. The only two times we got to ride in white people's cars were when we were picked up and taken to their fields to chop or pick cotton, and on Election Day.

Election days always presented a strange phenomenon because the behavior of many whites, especially those running for office, was so different. The same cars that passed and left you in a cloud of dust every day before stopped and offered you a ride on this day, and the driver made sure you knew who he was and whom he was supporting in the election. The next day, it was back to the same routine of passing and leaving you in a cloud of dust.

Although Selmer was like many southern towns in most ways, to those of us who lived there, it was different because we knew the stories of the past and lived the present ones daily. We walked the two and a half miles to school barefooted in the summer and freezing cold in the winter. We studied from books with missing covers and torn pages. We warmed ourselves by a coal stove, which burned you up front while you were still freezing on the backside. Add the urine smell of an unfortunate child that didn't make it to the toilet in time, if he even had one.

Many of my childhood experiences have become a source of shame for me, leaving scars that lasted for years. Not only was I ashamed of being so poor, I was ashamed of my own parents in many ways for the way they talked and their limited education. I was ashamed for them to meet our teachers, because they did not speak in a way that the teacher had drilled into us to speak. I was ashamed when other children made fun of us for having so many children in the family.

I did not realize that I lived a very sheltered life in Selmer. We went to school with all black students, we had all black teachers. We went to an all black church, worked in the fields with our family and friends, and that was about it.

When we did venture into the town of Selmer proper, it was to buy something, which was often an experience within itself. We were spoken to harshly by the clerk or at best in a condescending manner. They took your money and threw the change back on the counter making sure to never touch you. It made you feel contaminated. There was a little country store near our house, across highway 45, run by Old Man Defosters. It had a strange smell and there was always a group of older white men sitting around in front of or inside the store. They seemed to take pleasure at having fun at the expense of black children who came there.

Over the years, I've grown to appreciate what my parents were really like and what they had to do for us, and this has given me a great deal of pride. They did what they could, with what they had, under the circumstances. That is why I have chosen to call this book *Ollie's Kids*. This title was chosen not because I was raised by my mom alone; in fact, my mom and dad were married for over fifty years, and never separated until her death in 1976. But I selected this title because of her passion for her children, their safety, education, and religion. Each of these made a deep impression on me. I had a burning passion to share my feelings. The old folks around my home would say of a young person, "It's in him and it has to come out." After over sixty years, I still cannot get rid of this burning desire to tell this story because I wanted people to know about this little 5'3" black woman, with a mixture of American Indian and white blood in her veins, who appeared to be so ordinary but was so extraordinary. I am convinced there were thousands like her who had so little, without a decent house or modern conveniences. With nothing before her but the promise of hard work, and with nine children, she made it anyway. There are more like her who made it too.

Going to Town from School

Although our school was situated less than half a mile from the heart of Selmer, it was off limits for students to go to town during school hours. Occasionally a teacher or the principal would send a responsible student into town on an errand with the admonition: "You go right there and come straight back." A failure to follow these directions meant that you would not be sent on such an errand in the future.

The details of this road taken on the trip to town remain clear in my mind. Receiving the note for that errand, I walked proudly down the hall and out and down to the dirt road, going east to the main road into town. I would pass John Chamber's house on the right, which faced the Church of Christ's plain white building on the opposite side of the road.

As this road ran into the main road, the Methodist church building sat directly in front of you, before you made a left turn into town. A short distance, about midway into town, you would cross a narrow bridge running over Cypress Creek, where only one car at a time could cross. I remembered crossing that bridge as a smaller child, and how my mother held a viselike grip on my wrist as we made our way hurriedly across.

After crossing the bridge, we passed Zelphia Westbrook's café. Our parents would never let us go there because that was where lower class people hung out. They played pool, smoked cigarettes, cursed, played bad music on the jukebox, and occasionally got into fights. It was off limits for us, so we quickened our pace as we walked by, thinking one of those bad people might mess with us.

Crossing the nearby railroad to the left, we walked east along the track, and then we walked the remainder of the way to Highway 45 in the middle of Selmer, which was also the main street.

Bill told us a story from years earlier, when the McNairy County High School was just a Junior High School. Somehow he had heard that the Browder's Dry Good Store had socks on sale for five cents a pair. Since his socks had holes where they were not supposed to be, he really wanted a pair of those socks. The problem was, where was he going to get the nickel? There was only one source: Dad. Dad did not have much money, and he did not give up his money easily.

Bill had to work through Mom. Convincing her was not hard because the holed socks were in evidence. Moving to the next level, getting the money from Dad, was not so easy, but she was willing to try.

When Dad arrived home and got settled, Mom made her move. "Henry," she began, "this boy needs some socks real bad. She got nothing by way of reply, so she repeated herself, adding, "And they have some at Browder's or five cents a pair."

Dad mumbled something about the lack of money, and went off to bed with no commitment made. The next morning before the kids left for school, Mom was right back on the issue.

"Henry, this boy needs socks. They have them at Browder's for a nickel. It is time for the kids to go to school, are you going to give him the money or not?"

Turning his back, Dad unsnapped his little, black, lengthy purse that he always kept out of sight. He handed Bill the five-cent piece.

"Now go get those socks," he said.

Bill could hardly wait till school was out that day. He immediately made a beeline toward Broward's store. On his way, as he crossed the bridge over the creek, it occurred to him that it might be embarrassing to take off his worn socks in the store to put on the new ones. Without another thought he took his old socks off and threw them into the creek, watching them float away.

Hurrying on he could hardly wait to get to Browder's. Walking up to the counter he told the clerk, "I want a pair of those five-cent socks."

"I'm sorry," the clerk replied, "but that sale ended yesterday. We're sold out of those."

Bill always ended this story with how disappointed he was by not getting those socks. He never said what he did with the nickel or what he did for socks the next day.

Around the Dinner Table

We were taught that if you were visiting around mealtime at a neighbor's house and they invited you to eat, your reply was to always be "No thank you." This was because they were probably like our family and only had enough for themselves. Just think, if eight or nine hungry children came, unexpectedly, to your dinner table? We knew that they invited us as a courtesy, but we declined the invitations out of good manners.

This was not always easy, but we knew Mom's rules. You simply did not eat at other people's house unless you were invited, as a special guest, ahead of time. I remember how good a pot of beans or greens smelled. The aroma of fried chicken, ham or fish cooking, often made our mouths water and our stomachs growl, but you knew better than to yield to the temptations and say "yes."

We had a special order of eating at our house. Dad sat at the head of the table and Mom sat at the other end, the older children sat on one side and us younger children sat on a bench on the other side. Dad made the bench, and probably that table too.

Without plates, us smaller kids ate from the tin lids that came from the top of one-gallon cans of lard used by Mom. We had a few plates in the house, but they were reserved for adults and company. These plates were nothing fancy, often cracked or chipped in places, but for us they were the "special" dinner plates.

Mom would put down the food, steaming hot, on the table and Dad always said the blessing. I still remember it clearly: "Gracious Lord smile upon us, make us truly thankful for what we are about to receive. Amen." I often thought if God had given us the food, why did He have to make us thankful, but I would not dare raise that question, especially at that time.

Then Dad took the big bowl of the main course first, passing it around to Mom next. By the time it got to us we knew we had better take what we could get away with because it would not be around a second time. If one was reluctant about eating a piece of chicken or pie they would be asked, "Are you going to eat that?" and the next second someone would be reaching for it.

At our house, we learned strategies for eating. I remember one of mine. Whenever we had buttermilk, I enjoyed it with hot cornbread; I would ask for the cornbread early in the meal, chug it into my milk with plans to eat it later. This assured me of making certain to be good and full. Dad got wise to my plan and said, "If you ate that milk and cornbread you might be full." After repeating this a few more times, I realized that my plan was blown and dropped this routine. I've still been known to indulge the recipe from time to time.

One thing that I was not too proud of: my demeanor at the table when I was still a lap baby. My mother said each time I came to the table, I became extremely anxious before the blessing was asked. Every time in my excitement, I would lunge for the food, bumping my head on the table. Maybe it was a sign of my future behavior. It could have influenced why I have a hard head at times or possibly my excitement when I get an idea and want to implement it right away. This has caused me to often not think things through, as I should, before taking an action. Or it could have just meant I was a hungry baby.

With all of our hard times, I can say that we never went to bed hungry, and we never stole anything to have enough food to eat. We may have complained many times about the quality of our food, but looking back, we can see and realize that our mom and dad gave us the best they had. A lot of wisdom and love was shared around that kitchen table.

The Urge to Run

I always remember that whenever we encountered a group of white youth, it was our inclination to run. Although you had the feeling that you would love to stay and fight, the reality behind running was that if you fought and won, in the long run, you still lost. Whites could make you pay in so many ways. You could be moved if you lived in a house that belonged to them, or be denied the privilege of farming their land, or be marked as "uppity." Most of the time it seemed better to run to avoid a fight.

On Highway 45 running through Selmer, it was a form of recreation for us to sit on the bank by the side of the road and watch the cars go by. Often we would claim a pretty one as ours, and yell out, "My car!"

This activity was always exciting around Memorial Day. On or just before this day, we would see many cars from northern states heading to Shiloh National Park Cemetery, to honor their Civil War vets buried there. It was not uncommon to see cars from Ohio, Michigan, Illinois, Indiana, and Pennsylvania driving through Selmer on their way to Shiloh. At our school, we went to Shiloh Park many times, getting charged a fee to raise money for our clubs. As these cars cruised by, we claimed them. We also felt a tinge of pride because we realized that their ancestors likely were the guys who fought against slavery in the South.

On one such day, as we sat on the high banks claiming cars, a group of white boys stopped their car, got out and ran toward us. Although we had done nothing to them, when the older boys with me began to run, I ran too, unsure of why. They never caught up with us, because we had a head start. Even though I ran, I resented it, because there was no reason to run. It was a compilation of incidents like this one that gave me the urge to fight back. Although I never got into a fist fight with other boys, resentment began to build in me as I later learned to fight back in other ways.

The Spelling Match

Whenever we all got together, we could talk about being poor. The oldest siblings always insisted that they had it much worse than the younger ones.

Bill would have to win the prize with his spelling match story. He was an extremely bright little boy, so naturally, when it came time for a spelling bee in school, he was one selected for the competition. There was no problem with his spelling, but there was a problem with his shoes. The soles were worn out of the shoes, and the soles of his feet were touching the ground.

Fortunately, someone had given Mom a box of clothes. Out of this box came some shoes that were well worn. Bill found some that fit but each was only for the left foot. His only option was to wear those shoes, which were obviously not mates. Not only did he wear those shoes, but he won the spelling match wearing them. I will always bow to that effort, and success, because I cannot top it.

Chapter 5

History Repeats Itself: Verble Mae and Flurice Atkins

I was a still little boy when it happened, so I do not know the details of how this marriage came about. I faintly remember Mom sending me somewhere, likely to the store, with Verble, and I remember Flurice Atkins, her soon-to-be husband, standing by the roadside. I do not remember what, if anything was said.

Later that day, Verble was gone and Ollie was upset. Someone knew that Verble had run off, much like Mom had done years earlier and gotten married to Flurice, and then she later told our parents. I do remember her coming back to see us several days later, and I will always remember the little hat, a tam o'shanter; she wore on the side of her head.

I am certain that they did not think her husband Flurice was a proper boyfriend or husband because, although we all lived in Selmer, his family was not close to ours. He was also not a member of the Church of Christ.

As it later turned out, Verble and Flurice made the perfect match. He blended well with the family, treated Verble with respect, and became one of Ollie's favorite sons-in-law.

Flurice was a multitalented person, who had been born into a single parent family with a number of younger brothers and sisters. This man could do everything: cook, cut hair, drive any type of vehicle, swim, play games, and everyone seemed to like him. He was well balanced with a good sense of humor. He and Verble made an ideal couple, who worked together and seldom differed.

Years later, I asked Verble why she ran away and got married at that age. "Well Calvin," she replied, "I saw no hope or future by staying at home. We were always poor, and I saw no chance of going further in school."

Personally, I always felt that it was a shame that she could not go to school because she was always an exceptionally bright child and smarter still as a woman.

Coming from a challenging childhood, Flurice was still a kind, hard working, caring man and all that a husband could be. When Mom and the other members of the family got to know him, they soon forgave him and Verble for marrying so young. They soon settled in their own two-bedroom house, less than a mile from our family home.

A short while later, Flurice became a Christian, and later a leader in the local Church of Christ. When I became a teenage preacher, shortly after they got a car, Flurice took me to a number of places to preach.

Verble became a good cook. Sometimes Mom would be a little resentful when we would visit home, and we would pass her house and go straight to Verble's. We would always come back to Mom's house, after having had a good meal. If we went to their house and they were not cooking, we would wait until they cooked. Cooking was not Mom's gift. She would rather go to the field anytime than to prepare the meal for the workers.

Though she was never a birth mother, Verble was a "mother" to many of her own brothers and sisters. Vernell always claimed Herbert as her son, as they both were lighter complexioned, and Verble claimed me as hers, since we were the same shade of brown. All of the brothers and sisters loved Verble because her house was our home away from home.

Mom especially liked riding to church with Verble and Flurice after we left home. She also went many other places with them. As it turned out, Verble and Flurice proved to be more helpful to the rest of the family, and especially Mom and Dad, than any of the other children.

Although Verble only finished the seventh grade, she could have easily been mistaken for a college graduate if one heard her talk. Every word was in place, clearly enunciated, and with ideas clearly expressed. She taught Bible classes for many years for students of all ages, and she was a natural leader of women.

Talking with her during one of our long talks on a trip home I asked, "Why were you so aggressive and ready to stand up for yourself and others when you felt mistreated?"

"When I was a little girl," she said, "Bill, always called me Kokomo and dared me to do many things. When I started to being so aggressive, I found that people respected you more when you stood up and spoke up for yourself."

She was stopped in her tracks though, literally, when she decided to try driving her husband's car. When she put the car in reverse she backed into a tree. Flurice did not scold her, nor force her to try again right away. It was a long time before she would ever try to drive again.

Verble brought her characteristic aggressiveness to her work that she showed in other areas of life. Her first work after marriage was in the field as a sharecropper with her husband. I remember seeing her chopping cotton in their rented field looking quite lonely while the rest of us worked together in our field. She never had a job making a great deal of money. As a cook and waitress at the Sunset Inn her salary was exactly zero, working with her husband for the white Baptist Church paid very little, and finally working at a local motel paid them just enough to live on. She retained this job following the death of Flurice, and in spite of these meager jobs, she always managed to give faithfully in church and to assist other worthy causes.

Flurice Would Not Take It

Flurice had an old car, a Chevrolet that had been remodeled into a truck. If you sat in the back you could dangle your legs off, like a flat bed.

One day, Herbert and I were riding with Flurice coming home. A car filled with white kids passed and immediately cut back in front of us, clipping his front bumper. We felt the hit. The car stopped after pulling over, and Flurice pulled up right behind them, grabbed a large screwdriver from the glove compartment, ready to fight, and whatever else needed to be done, if he needed to do so.

To our surprise, the young white boys apologized, right away, and asked if there was any damage to our car. Fortunately, there was none. I felt glad that there was no fight, but I felt good to see my brother-in-law stand up like a man. I also learned a very important lesson that day: If you are mistreated, and you stand up ready to fight, you might not have to fight.

Dorothy Found the Whiskey

We walked about two and a half miles to and from school each day. The trip to school was uneventful because we had to arrive no later than 8:30 a.m. But the trip home allowed us to enjoy the scenery, play with each other, and explore the landscape.

One place of interest was the "Junk Pile," a place where service stations and other businesses would dump their junk down a big hill into a hollow of waste. Sometimes fire would be burning cardboard boxes, wood, or greasy rags. I was reminded of it later, when I learned about Gehenna.

This junk pile was fascinating for us to explore. Occasionally, we would find something of value that we could use. It was not uncommon to find an old used tire.

This was not a day different from any other when we came to the junk pile. Then we saw that some store had just thrown out some new junk. As we got closer, we discovered that a truck had dumped a load of smashed whiskey bottles. Selmer was a dry county, where the sale of whiskey was illegal. If confiscated, it had to be destroyed. One can imagine the smell in that pile of junk. It was almost strong enough to make one feel drunk. Coming from a family where Mom despised even a drop of alcohol, we had only taken a sip when a "good ol'boy" had sold our dad a gallon of moonshine to break our measles out.

I often wondered why we needed a gallon, but knowing that my dad took an occasional "nip," I am sure he took care of the rest of it. Maybe he had a friend or two to help.

Nevertheless, that strange smell and the sight of new junk intrigued us. We could not wait to dig in, in spite the risk of getting cut on the smashed bottles. We soon realized that the search was useless and slowly began to move toward home. Dorothy lagged behind, still digging through the rubble, determined to find something worthwhile if it was there.

After we had gone down the dusty road a ways, she shouted out, "Look what I found!" The rest of us turned around and looked back. She stood holding a bottle of commercial grade whiskey. The seal on the bottle had not been broken.

"How did we miss that?" we all thought. But if anyone were going to find that bottle it would be Dorothy. I share this experience not because she was in any way inclined to drinking. I doubt she ever took a drink in her life. I share this to demonstrate her determination to go on when others quit. This was the spirit that defined her in life as she married and later raised her family.

Frankly, I do not know what ever happened to that whisky in the beautiful bottle. I have a slight suspicion that it must have landed in Dad's hands to "get it out of the hands of the children." There is no doubt what Mom would have done; she would have poured it down the drain (if we had a drain). Better yet, it would have ended up in the grass. Again, I don't remember seeing any drunken snakes slithering across the yard.

That Little Old Winemaker, Dad

Under no stretch of the imagination would Dad ever be called a drunk, but he was not above taking a drink or two at certain times. I only remember him actually getting drunk twice. One of those times was Christmas Eve, when our expectations of him were at the highest. Christmas morning, we got nothing because

Dad got with the wrong crowd that day and drank too much. These guys called him "Dandy." Maybe they didn't know what it meant, or had a different idea about what it meant. I did notice that this was a nickname was used mostly by the men in our family and close male friends.

The dictionary defines "dandy" as a man who gives exaggerated attention to dress or something excellent in class. Although Dad was proud of his second rate clothing that he wore on special occasions and call them his "vines," I never thought of him as a fancy dresser. He might have been if he could have been. More and more, I have come to think of him as the second part of the definition of "dandy." As something that is "excellent in its class."

Anyway, when he sobered up on Christmas Day, he was so embarrassed that I felt sorry for him and really wanted to say, *"That's okay Dad."* He got up and went to the local store, actually buying us more by way of presents than we would have gotten in the first place. Over the years, we mostly got fruit, candy, a few nuts, but hardly any toys. Actually, we did not miss out on much that year, which made forgiving him easier.

It was not uncommon in our neighborhood for people to make a little homemade wine. Sometimes it was called "home brew." Dad got the idea to make some for himself. He enlisted our help in picking blackberries to put in this barrel. After letting this set for a while, he strained the blackberries out and looked forward to enjoying some blackberry wine. I will never know why he needed a whole barrel of wine. Maybe it was because he wanted to share it with his friends. He was what was called a freehearted person, sharing vegetables and other things from the garden.

Incidentally, this wine barrel was at the barn, which was usually locked. After the blackening juice set for a while, he was ready to taste his new wine. Something was wrong, and all who tasted agreed that something was *very* wrong. We found out that the barrel that he had bought in town was previously a dill pickle barrel, and what Dad had made was beautiful purple vinegar. Did we have a laugh as we put purple vinegar over our peas, cabbage and other vegetables! We also shared vinegar with neighbors and friends. Sometimes we told them the story and sometimes we did not. One thing for sure, that put an end to Dad's attempts at winemaking.

Chattanooga

I will always remember how I learned to spell Chattanooga. I was sitting on a wagon alongside a machine made of iron and painted red, riding out to the fields. Cast into the iron were the words "Chattanooga Plow Comp'y." Fortunately, I already knew the correct spelling of "company."

It was the fall of the year, harvest time. In addition to picking cotton, pulling corn and harvesting potatoes and turnips, there was one more task that I will never forget; making molasses. My grandfather, the original Verdell, was considered to be one of the best molasses makers in the area. This was a detailed process that had to be carried out from start to finish that day.

It began with a good crop of sorghum cane. When it was full grown, the leaves had to be stripped from the cane while it was standing, and then the cane would be cut and put into neat piles. Both the leaves stripped from the cane and the seed heads cut from the top were tied into "hand" bundles, which were set aside to feed the cows.

Once the cane was delivered to the site where the molasses was to be made, it was time for the process to begin. A mule was hitched to the pole that turned the red mill, made in Chattanooga, Tennessee, and the cane was systematically placed between the turning rollers, which crushed the cane. The juice ran into a five-gallon can set beneath the mill, and the crushed cane, called "palmings," was constantly taken away. The fresh ground juice was poured into a gridded pan over a fire pit. With a special type of mop Grandpa moved the raw juice from grid to grid until it reached the last one where it actually became molasses.

Every person had a job to do in this process: bringing the cane to the wagon, feeding it into the mill (my job), taking away the palmings which would sometimes cut into your hand, taking the juice to the grid pan, and watching the five gallon can fill up with those golden molasses at the end. Seeing Grandpa do this one would know that he was a master of his trade. If you had any doubts, a taste of the molasses as they cooled would remove them.

Our breakfast often consisted of butter stirred in molasses, spread over biscuits with bacon, if we had bacon. We also used it to sweeten rice for dinner and grits for breakfast. You can see how Grandpa's molasses came in handy.

Our noon meal frequently consisted of cornbread made from the grist mill, peas or beans cooked with a piece of pork; nearly all of our meat consisted of pork, with an occasional chicken taken from the yard and killed. Add to this whatever was available from the garden, which could be mustard or turnip greens, yams, onions, cabbage or green beans. Seldom did we have any desert, like a cake or a pie.

The Sunset Inn

Major always wanted to be an entrepreneur. The best he could do was to find a job at a local grocery market as a meat cutter. With a small employee discount, he tried his hand at barbequing a part of a hog and selling barbeque sandwiches. This went well enough, since he sold all that he had.

Then he got a new idea that if he had a building, he could start his own café. Dad went along with the idea and helped him by building a nice place, across from the high school, on one of his lots. It had a kitchen, counters, and all the looks of a café. A day was set and an opening was planned.

We called the new café "The Sunset Inn." Our main menu consisted of hot dogs, hamburgers, and pickled pigs' feet. We also sold sodas, candy bars, peanuts, and a few other snacks. Of course we had a jukebox where you could play a favorite record for a nickel.

Our sister Verble was the main cook, and I brought in, on my bicycle, the hot dogs and hamburger meat, from the store where Major worked.

At the beginning, people flocked to our place, first because there was no other place, besides Zelphia's Café. Frankly, I do not remember Verble or me ever getting paid. There should have been some money being made somewhere. Major worked himself on weekends, after getting off from his regular job. People on all levels, out of curiosity or some other reason, accommodated us by dropping by.

Gradually, the lack of a long term business plan or strategy, caused our demise.

First of all, the high school principal made our place off-limits to students. I understood that was because of the possibility of students sneaking over there during school hours. That cut down on our business.

Secondly, Major's accounting system was far from the best. By putting the cash directly into his pocket, none of us, including him, knew what was being taken in, nor what was spent out. Adding to this was the fact that too many friends told him to "put it on the book," and they never paid. The outgo began to exceed the income.

Finally, from the experiences that I'd had personally, I vowed to get out of and never again go into the restaurant business. This was caused by one thing: fights!

I remember this one guy we will call "Jimmy," had it in for another guy we'll call "Buddy." On one occasion, when the place was crowded, Jimmy came in the backdoor with a crowbar and began hitting Buddy across the head. He fell to the floor, out cold. Several men grabbed Jimmy and wrestled him to the floor, while others carried Buddy out to the doctor. When the sheriff finally came, nobody knew anything about what had happened. I doubt if Jimmy went to jail. I realized at that point that we were not going to get much help from the police, especially when it was a black-on-black crime. This was a lesson that I was to learn over and over again.

There were other fights, some people got cut and others shot, but I do not remember anyone actually getting killed. These things were enough to give us a bad reputation though, and to take our business with it. Finally, we had to shut it down. Someone remarked at the time that the sun went down on the Sunset Inn. Really, I was glad and just wanted to move on.

The Return of Bill

Sometimes I think that tough times in Lexington left some marks on Bill. Based on some of the things he did after graduating from Lexington High, I feel that he may have felt ashamed of the poverty at home.

Graduating from high school, he went directly to Nashville and we didn't hear from him for a time. Finally, in 1942, when he was drafted into the army, Mom had the Red Cross look him up.

This started a flow of information from him, and out of his salary, he started sending twenty dollars per month to the family. This may sound meager, but it meant a great deal to us to have that extra twenty dollars coming in each month.

During a three-year period, he served in Europe and gained the rank of Staff Sergeant, and then he came home. We gave him a hero's welcome.

We heard that he had spent the night in Selmer before making the two-and-a-half mile trek to our house. The next morning Herbert and I had somewhere to go, I do not really recall where, but as we got about a half-mile up the road, we saw this uniformed figure walking slowly and stately toward us. As he got near, we could only grin, as we remained frozen in place. He spoke first.

Back at the house, we had a great celebration because we had not seen him in such a long time. The next day, we retrieved his trunk from the bus station in town. That was when the real excitement began. When he opened it, there seemed to be everything in it. There were gifts for everyone, and especially for Mom and Dad. I got a pair of wings to pin on my shirt, which made me very proud.

We were all amazed when Bill showed us the pair of $40 shoes, made in Belgium. We all admired them and handled them with the greatest care, because we had never paid more than $2.98 for shoes.

Bill stayed around about thirty days, and that was when we really got to know him. He showed us many pictures with German and French men and women. He also shared his exploits with white women, which fueled Herbert's and my imaginations.

He slicked down our hair with Murray Pomade and took us to a Saturday night movie. It was a western featuring Gene Autry. We never forgot that movie.

I remember him telling us about World War II ending in Europe. He said, "On that night, everybody got drunk." Then my mother asked, "Son, did you get drunk?" Then he repeated, "I said, <u>everybody</u> got drunk." There was a great silence and Mom never mentioned it again.

Several days later, he went to school with us. He looked so great in his uniform with his sergeant stripes. We were proud to show him off. My friends began to tease me and call me "General Eisenhower's brother." I did not mind; in fact, I rather liked it.

Before leaving, he taught us how to dance as we listened to the radio. I especially remember one song that he liked, which had come from Europe, *Symphony*, sung by Johnny Desmond. I still think of him when I occasionally hear it.

After that first major visit, we looked forward to his coming home every three years, between his re-enlistments. On one occasion, he wired our house for electricity and actually had the lights turned on. This made a huge difference in our lives. Our home was never the same with electric lights. Bill gave us all inspiration with his great stories and gifts.

After twenty years of this routine and his retirement from the army, once again he settled in Nashville and married Bea, the love of his life. He began working in security for a local bank where he spent many years. He also had his own business on the side, as an electrician, which extended beyond his days at the bank.

During his time in Nashville, he became the father of two children, Greg and Angelita. He enjoyed his life with Bea and his part-time work as an electrician.

It was my privilege to visit him in Nashville a number of times, where we also had a great time visiting and reminiscing, with plenty of laughs.

Ollie's Love of Music

Another form of recreation for Mom came through her love of music. Her singing was mainly limited to acapella in church. Occasionally she would sing a hymn or spiritual while doing her work around the house.

Every Saturday night, she never missed the Grand Ole Opry, which came on radio station WSM from Nashville. Before we had a radio, they would go to my sister's house down the road on Saturday night. Finally, we got our own battery powered Sonara radio, which was a big step up for us.

Mom's favorite singer was Roy Acuff, who was famous for singing *The Great Speckled Bird* and *The Wabash Cannonball*. When he came on, we had to be quiet since she hung on every word of his songs. Acuff eventually ran for Governor of Tennessee, and although he lost, I am sure she voted for him. Roy Acuff had a comic sidekick named Oswald who would bray like a mule after a joke. We all got a laugh out of that and waited for it each week.

Mom's second favorite singer was Ernest Tubbs, who had a distinct low-key voice and a Texas drawl. His most popular song was *Walking the Floor Over You*, which he seemed to sing every week. I later learned that he did have other songs.

As long as I can remember, we always had a guitar in the house. Dad played it fairly well and tried to sing along with his strumming. I am glad he kept his day job. But that was another side of him that we all enjoyed.

Mom could play one or two songs on the guitar, but she never sang as she played. Her strumming on the guitar was very gentle, and I remember trying to learn the song she played. I could not get anything resembling a musical sound when I put my fingers on the strings. Even today, I get the urge to go to the music department of a community college and take a lesson on guitar. Maybe I will live out this fantasy sometime in the future. I did, however, learn to play one or two tunes on the piano, but a Little Richard or an Errol Garner I was not, and was not meant to be.

Practicing Prejudice Against a Pig

Uncle Dave gave my mother, Ollie, a sow. We were delighted and excited when she had eight or nine pigs in her first litter. We immediately claimed our favorite ones. All were claimed except this one, which had a brownish red color with black spots. Although she had no control of her color, we didn't like her and called her "Mingley." We excluded Mingley in every possible way as we showed affection to all of the other pigs. One day, for no apparent reason, we started chasing Mingley. We were just having fun at her expense. To our surprise, we found Mingley dead the next day. We all were sad and felt a great deal of guilt. We thought, *"What made us do what we did for no cause?"* This poor little pig had been the victim of prejudice.

Many times when I have been the victim of prejudice I thought about Mingley. Why in the world do I have to suffer like this just because of my color, over which I have no control? Why do people dislike me who do not even know my name?

I have often reflected on what was said by Kyle Haselden in his book on *The Racial Problem in Christian Perspective.* "Discrimination," he says, "denies my right to have. Segregation denies my right to belong and stereotyping denies my right to be." What a price to pay, just for being who you are.

Not only is racism painful to its victim, but it is equally harmful to those who perpetrate it. It extends the myth that one is superior to another. Peter said, "Of a truth I perceive that God is not respecter of persons: but in him and worketh righteousness is accepted by him," Acts 10:34-35

The Tragedy that Brought Us a Car

When I was about ten, I remember Principal Professor Gray coming to our classroom and calling me to come out. Much to my surprise, all of the rest of my brothers and sisters were waiting outside also. He told us that we needed to go home because there had been a death in the family. Our Uncle Troy, Mom's youngest brother, who had lived in Humboldt, Tennessee, was on his way to Nashville with a group of three other men, when they had made a wrong turn and the car crashed into the side of a mountain. All were killed. That was a sad day for us.

I distinctly remember Uncle Troy. He was a tall, slender, light-skinned man, with a pleasant smile. He brought his wife, Aunt Clevester, his daughter Geraldine and his son G. Roy, when he came to see us; we were always glad to see them, and hated to see them leave. I remember once, G. Roy was sitting in the front seat of the car and honking the horn. Uncle Troy simply came out and gave him a gentle shake of his head but said nothing. I liked this gentle man who did not speak harshly. Now he was gone. Ollie cried all night. I wanted ease her sorrow, but we could not stop her crying. The next morning she was quieted some and began to realize that she would have to go to Humboldt, about fifty miles away.

As they made ready for the funeral and Mom prepared to go, Aunt Clevester made a startling announcement. She wanted to give Uncle Troy's car, a 1930 Chevrolet, to Major. That was a surprise, giving a car to a seventeen-year-old boy who could not drive a lick. But he soon learned.

I remember Mom got George Gardner to go to Humboldt to drive the car home, and I remember our excitement when he drove up in our yard. We could hardly believe that we actually had a car.

Just about that time, George Estes, a local white boy of Major's age, who had played with him and other boys their age, rode up on his bicycle. He looked the car over and carefully inspected it. As he rode away, he said loud enough for us all to hear him, "He will knock every mud hole dry now." Major did just that and we rode with him whenever we could.

Fair Weather Friends

Major was the only boy in school with a car. Everyone wanted to ride, especially the girls. The boys saw it as a way they could go see girls in Bethel, Purdy and Ramer. They would usually nickel and dime up to pay for gas.

One night, around nine o'clock, Major was not home and Mom was worried. She imagined all kinds of things that could have happened to her boy. When it got to be midnight, she was really worried. Major did not come home all night, and by then, all of us were worried.

About eight or nine the next morning, Major came driving up. He explained, "I got stuck in a mud hole with my friends in the car and ran out of gas trying to get out." His friends laughed at him for the longest as he tried to start that car all through the night. They were probably the very ones who had not nickel and dimed up.

Somehow he got gas, and got that car out of the mud hole, but this was just one of several incidents with his car when his friends were of no help to him. Major eventually learned what kinds of friends they were: the fair weather kind.

Chapter 6

Herbert, My Leader

I BELIEVE I WAS CLOSER TO Herbert than any other sibling in the family. Being about three years older than me, he had a major influence on my life. I cannot remember a time when he was not there, with a natural instinct to protect me. With this protection also came control. Naturally, there were times he got us both into trouble, but overall, the good outweighed the bad.

When we were both too young to go to the fields, we wandered through the woods near our house, exploring. He was an adventurous and natural leader. I was a natural follower. He taught me how to climb trees, avoid poison ivy, and to know which wild berries were good to eat. He also taught me when to run and when to stay and fight.

One day, we saw this turtle in a creek of clear running water. The water was shallow and we could wade right in barefooted. To us, this turtle meant food on the table. I watched Herbert reach into the water slowly and catch the turtle by the tail. When it bit the stick placed before it, this meant its head would be cut off and soon our family enjoyed turtle soup for dinner thanks to Herbert's ingenuity.

We both went fishing with Mom sometimes, but actually we never caught many fish. Our goal was not fishing for fun but for food.

I remember Herbert getting into trouble. He was not a mean person, nor was he ever in trouble with law enforcement, but his curiosity and willingness to try new things ended up getting him into some unpleasant situations.

There was the time when he ended up having to go to the local clinic for about fourteen consecutive days to get rabies shots in his stomach, because of our dog which might have bitten him. Our parents took no chances. They found the money to pay for the shots and ended up killing the dog, even though the dog may not have had rabies.

Dad told Jewell our youngest sister to take a water bucket to Herbert to get water from the spring. When she gave him the bucket, he thumped her ear real hard. She let out a cry and cried all the way back to the house to make sure Dad heard her. When Herbert returned with the water, the old man was waiting, with a well-trimmed switch. He gave Herbert a good whipping, talking as he whipped. We teased Herbert for months about one of the things Dad said: "You had to thump the baby's ear!" The rest of us, along with cousin "Son Baby," got a big laugh each time we reminisced about this.

Another time, Major, always the entrepreneur was selling Keystone products, which included a hair dressing for men and facial powders and toiletries for women. All the products were distinctly for people of color. Herbert, when commissioned by Major, showed no respect of a person's color and stopped by the homes of several white families, and actually sold some of the products to white girls. We had a big laugh about Herbert's daring ways, but Major refused to increase his commission.

We were never a fighting family, among ourselves or with those outside the family. It may have been due to the double penalty system used by our mother. If you happened to get into a fight, you had better win. If you lost you could get up to three whippings for the one incident. One from the person you were fighting, a second from the teacher, another when you arrived home. The emphasis always seemed to be on tearing up your clothes more than the fact that you could get hurt.

I never remembered Herbert getting into many fights, other than several skirmishes with Rosie and Dorothy. There was the time when I thought that I might be able to whip him. With a pair of work gloves and being egged on by Major, I attacked him with relentless aggression. He felt it alright, but so did I when he threw and hit me with an icy snowball upside the head. My ear felt glued to my head. Although I did not cry, I certainly remembered my place in the pecking order.

They Called Me "Doc"

It was common for neighbors to claim certain children as their favorite. Herbert was Mr. Sam Peter's favorite and he called him "Peter Rabbit." I don't know if he liked it or not, but he never complained.

I was the favorite of Mr. McMann and his wife, Miss Maude. They rewarded me in many ways, like the time Mr. McMann bought me a battery-powered little red car, with bright lights. They began to call me "Doc." I liked the name, and somewhere along the way I wanted to become a real doctor. Soon, everybody was calling me "Doc." This has persisted for years, so to this day, my nieces, nephews, and my late wife's sisters still call me "Doc."

Herbert and His Shadow

Herbert was left-handed, like me. I've often wondered if I wound up left-handed because of his influence. I will never know, but this proved quite convenient in a number of situations. We matched up at the dining room table, sawing wood together with a crosscut saw, playing basketball, and a number of other situations.

We were kids with great imaginations. Whenever we read comic books, listened to the radio or just watched people, we imagined how they lived beyond what we saw or heard. How would Tom Mix deal with a crooked sheriff? How would Red Ryder handle a gang of roughnecks trying to take over the town? Roy Rogers, Gene Autry, and the Lone Ranger all had a place in our imaginary world. We borrowed secondhand comic books and lived the lives of the heroes found in them. Later, it occurred to me that I was always in the role of the sidekick. Herbert was the Red Ryder and I was Little Beaver, I was the Tonto to his Lone Ranger. We will still have to talk about this because I need some answers.

Actually, television was almost an invasion of our imagination because of the realities it brought. A good time for us was a rainy day where we went into the hayloft and ate peanuts right off the dry vines stored there. We talked about the girls we liked and the girls we thought liked us. We talked about the exploits of our heroes in the comic books and all the other funny things we could think of.

I distinctly remember the first movie Herbert went to see, *Meet Me in St. Louis*, with Margaret O'Brien and Judy Garland. The next day while we were clearing a ditch bank, he reenacted the movie to me in great detail. Although I never saw the movie, I still remember all of the details and the stars who played in it.

As we grew up, one major thrill for Herbert and me was going to the movies on Saturday night. We would see a movie about one of our cowboy heroes, *Red Ryder*, *Hopalong Cassidy*, Gene Autry, the *Lone Ranger*, or Tom Mix, and there would also be a serialized short, ending in a cliffhanger to get you back in the following week.

Always lurking in your mind as you enjoyed the movie was the two-and-a-half mile walk home after the movie was over. The walk coming to the movie theater never seemed nearly as long as the walk home. Discussing the highlights of the movie made the walk somewhat more bearable.

On this particular Saturday night when the movie ended, we began the trek home. Just as we were approaching a huge hill, a big flatbed lumber truck passed us. We wished that the driver would have offered us a ride, but he chugged on by. The hill was steep and the truck almost came to a stop, straining to make the hill. I suppose the temptation was too great, because before I knew it, Herbert was running and jumping up onto the back end of the truck. What was I to do? I had to decide in a split second. Since the truck was nearing the top of the hill and Herbert was already on it, it was an easy decision for me to catch up and get on too. As we rode those two and a half miles, it was a pleasant thought to realize that we would get home early.

But as we got closer to our destination a number of questions faced us: Did the truck driver know that we were on the back of his truck? If he stopped, would he have been hostile and harm us? What about the fork in the road that was coming up? Was he going toward Falcon or toward Highway 45? Finally, would the driver be going downhill, on level ground, or uphill when it was time for us to get off?

Actually, when it came time for us to get off it became obvious to us that he was going south toward Falcon, not the way we wanted to go. It also seemed at that point, he began going slightly downhill and speeding up a bit. Herbert jumped. Once again, I was left alone facing a decision. I had to jump, and when I did for a few minutes my head spun around as I gained my composure. The life threatening aspect came to me as I reflected on the possibility of another car driving closely behind the truck. I never think of that incident without having that thought. Herbert and I still laugh about it and sometimes say, "We never should have caught that truck."

There were no doubts in my mind that Herbert was Dad's favorite son. Maybe it was because Herbert was born as Dad was growing older, but it also could have been because he was such a handsome little boy or smart little boy who could help out with Dad's work. Whatever it was, he was the one that went with Dad the most and seemed to enjoy it. Therefore, he accumulated a number of stories about Dad that I never knew about, at least first hand.

Mrs. Nina May Latta was the wife of the owner of the Ford Motor Car Company of Selmer. She was also a member of the

Church of Christ, and we were sharecroppers on their land for several years. She also liked the carpentry work that Dad did, probably because he was very skilled, and also cheap, charging only fifty cents an hour. Often Dad took Herbert with him as he worked for her. She also took a liking to Herbert when he was a teenager and began to have him work for her. She also took him around as she visited other sites owned by her family. Herbert liked this because it gave him insights into the private ways that middle-class white families lived, insights that would be valuable throughout his life.

Herbert liked girls and girls like him. In spite of the fact that we were poor, it seemed that he always managed to come up with attractive clothes: a colorful shirt, a new pair of pants, or a new cap. Although I liked some of the girls who liked him, they had their minds set on older boys. Most of the time, I never got a second look from them because I was "Herbert's little brother." He would tell me about his experiences of dating girls, which only fueled my young imagination.

In May of 1949, it was time for Herbert to graduate from high school. The end of the school year was always a bittersweet time for us with friends graduating and missing the routine of school and being with classmates. On the other hand, we enjoyed the feeling of freedom from the classroom to do new things. Moving on was always tinged with sadness.

Herbert's graduation was especially sad to me. I realized that our relationship would be changing. He would be going somewhere, and I would be left alone. He sang a solo at his graduation, "I've Done My Work." As I looked at him, I almost began to cry and thought to myself, "*A young man like that ought to have a chance to become all that he can be."* Like an eagle in the sky, he circled the home environment several times and within a few months, he was gone.

Snipe Hunting

Major, was always playing tricks on the younger kids in the family. Herbert and I were his favorite targets. He proudly announced, "I am going to take you boy's snipe hunting tonight." He led us to believe that a snipe was a bird, much like a quail, that made a delicious meal. We were anxious to go. We were quite used to him going hunting and trading us parts of the animals (rabbit, opossums, or squirrels) before they were trapped or killed. We were convinced that we would have a wonderful meal in store.

To hunt snipe, we would need large grass sacks. We called them "tote" sacks. The snipe flocked around the ditch bank at nights, according to Major. All we had to do was to stand at the spot at the ditch bank with our sacks open to catch them. Meanwhile, he would go down the ditch and drive them up for us to catch. We imagined going home with a bag filled with birds.

We fell for the trick, hook, line, and sinker. The only problem was that the snipes never came and Major never came back. We finally realized something was fishy about this plan. The only snipes out that night were two silly little boys who had been tricked again by their older brother. Major got great joy out of repeating the snipe-hunting story. We did not like it at all.

Dorothy's Friends

Dorothy was a beautiful brown-skinned girl, fun-loving with a bit of mischievousness in her eyes. If she were not saying something funny she was thinking about it. Naturally, people were attracted to her, especially the boys. Although I only remember one boyfriend of Rosie, I distinctly remember three for Dorothy, not counting Tee Spence whom she married in 1947.

Actually, I do not know if Marcus Campbell could really be called a boyfriend. He was from Ramer, Tennessee, about twenty miles away. He had somehow met and talked with Dorothy and evidently made a date to come see her. He got a man by the name of Lacy Chambers, whom the family knew, to bring him to Selmer on a Sunday afternoon.

After church we were all Verble's house. Whenever a car turned off the main road to our house it always brought a burst of excitement from us younger children. As it came closer we recognized its passengers as Lacy and Marcus.

Lacy got out and greeted us all and proceeded to the house talking to the family sitting on the porch as he went. Marcus got out but stood around the car until Dorothy emerged from the house and went out to greet him. Mom had her eye on him from time he arrived. When they opened the door of the car and sat down inside, Mom made her move. Walking slowly but deliberately, as if she were thinking about what to say, she went straight to the car. As children, this was an exciting moment and we were not about to miss a word. Speaking first to Dorothy she said, "Dorothy, come in the house."

Our hearts stood still because we did not know what Dorothy's response would be. Before Dorothy could move Mom turned to Marcus and said, "She is not old enough to have company." As Dorothy got out of the car, Mom turned and walked slowly away without saying another word.

When Dorothy got out of the car and walked toward the house, Marcus' eyes followed her until she disappeared. Then he turned to us and said, "Well I guess I had better call up Lacy," and he honked the horn. Lacy appeared in the door and said, "Did you want something?" "Yes," Marcus replied. "Okay, I will be right there," he said as he walked down the steps of the porch. They got in the car and drove away and I never knew the rest of the story.

After Marcus there was Willard Lutrell, who lived in Old Purdy, about five miles away. He, along with his sister, Cozell, and brother, Waymon, all attended McNairy County High School at one time or another. Willard must have been several years older than Dorothy and several grades ahead of her in school. Most of the time they dated he was in the military. It appeared to be serious because the letters came and went on a regular basis.

Being a military sweetheart had many dimensions. Carrying on a courtship from afar reduced the social pressures from being around each other too frequently. It also had an element of national loyalty since the one being dated was serving his country and the girl felt she was supporting the war effort. Finally, it provided a measure of security for not being bothered by those who made social advances. One could always say, "My sweetheart is in the military."

Willard was a quiet, serious young man who seemed very dignified in every respect. He was most mannerly to older people and younger children. When he was in school, the teachers respected him because he was a good student. But all of this did not seem quite right for the personality of Dorothy, who was an energetic, lively person. Far away was fine, but close up was a different story.

While Willard was away in the military, another young man entered the picture. His name was Frank Walker and he had moved to Selmer from Decaturville, Tennessee, about forty miles away. Frank had a car and worked at a local service station. He was a handsome young man who was friendly but a bit shy.

Frankly, I do not believe that Dorothy ever got too serious with him. There was always a sense of, "This relationship is over once my real boyfriend comes home." But it did not turn out exactly that way. When there was no longer a "Military Mystique," Willard seemed more ordinary with no well-defined future and the relationship began to wane.

To hurry the process along was a fellow from Corinth, Mississippi, just across the state line, named Tee Spence. I really do not know how he met Dorothy, but once he did his persistence finally won her over. Tee was like her Mr. Everything as he got to know the whole family and embraced them.

I remember Tee coming to our house during the week when it was too wet to work in the field, and Dad was unloading hay at the barn. He jumped right in and began helping. He offered to pick us all up and take us to Corinth to meet his family, who turned out to be very friendly. They owned a large farm, lived in a nice house, and had a big garden, with chickens and ducks running all over the place. Dad did not go to Corinth, but the rest of us were very impressed.

Several weeks later, Tee came to our house and Willard was there. He had no car so someone else had brought him. Tee greeted him with open arms and was quite friendly toward him. In fact when someone suggested going for a ride, Tee volunteered to drive, inviting Willard and Dorothy to go along. They accepted.

When they stopped at a store for snacks Willard went in to get them. While he was in the store, Tee asked Dorothy, "When can I come to see you again?" When she agreed to let him come for a visit, he knew he was "in." It was also true that Willard was on his way out. It was not too long before the fire was burning between the two of them and wedding bells were coming.

I had one trip to Corinth, which was in my usual role, chaperone for a social event. As we made the seventeen-mile drive back from Corinth to our house, I knew things were getting serious and thought, *"This has to go into my report."* Little did I know that they were already planning to get married that weekend. When I got out of the car, they got out of the car and went into the house with me.

Mom and Dad were already in bed. After a few words Tee said, "I started to marry that girl tonight, but I thought I would wait until Saturday. Mom rose up and asked Dad, "Did you hear that Henry?" I do not remember the words of the conversation after that. I do know that Dorothy became Mrs. Tee Spence on March 23, 1947 in Corinth, Mississippi.

The Narrow Escapes of #8

I suppose everyone looks back one time or another at the time they could have lost their life. I have four that I distinctly remember.

The first incident I was told about many times by my mother. On this occasion, her mother, Sarah, had come to visit. She was proud of all of her grandchildren but the new one always got the most attention. I am certain at this time, that this was the case. Mom never told me my exact age at the time of this incident. It was at a time that I required lots of attention.

Grandmother Sarah enjoyed holding and feeding us. This time she was feeding me small cut up pieces of tomato. It happened that she made a mistake and gave me a piece that was too large for me to swallow and it lodged in my throat, choking me. After trying desperately to remove the tomato, grandmother had no choice but to report what was happening to my mother.

Handing my limp body to my mother, she said, sorrowfully, "Ollie, I have killed your baby." Ollie would have none of that and, acting instinctively, she immediately grabbed me, opened my mouth and ran her finger down my throat and got the chunk of tomato, and soon I was crying normally for more tomato. Needless to say, Grandmother Sarah was quite relieved and thankful. Mom would always finish this episode by saying, "I never blamed my mother for what happened."

This is not to give the reader the impression that I was always in trouble by being too adventuresome or taking unnecessary risks. I think that I was pretty normal with a simple childish curiosity about the world.

I do not remember my age, or all of the surrounding circumstance when I decided to put a pea in my ear. After a few seconds when the experiment was over, I tried to take it out, but it only went in further. At that point, it was lodged. My head began to roar and people sounded funny as they talked around me.

I panicked and maybe even cried. This got the attention of the whole household. Some of the siblings laughed at my stupidity, others scolded me and said I should have known better, but my mother took action. She tried to remove the pea, but it only went further into the ear. Giving up on her efforts she declared, "Henry, we are going to have to take this boy to the doctor. I do not remember how nor how soon we got to the doctor's office, but I was happy to get there.

After his usual questioning of how and what had happened he said sat me in a chair. As he came close and began to examine my ear, I recall the distinct smell of medicine, which I had detected when I first entered the office, which was more evident at that moment. He took out a variety of instruments and while continuing to talk he tried several of them. With a little tug, he pulled the pea out handed it to my mother and said, "Here is your pea." Boy, did I feel relieved as I looked at that pea! That relief was short lived as I received a scolding on my way back home and the scorn of being laughed at by my siblings when I arrived home. They never let me forget that incident. To this day I have nothing against peas, but I would rather see them on my plate well cooked than anywhere near my ear.

Of course, the truly frightening incidents usually involved Herbert. Somehow we got the idea one night to throw rocks on Mr. Phil Baxter's tin roofed house. I'm not sure why we started this. He was friend to our family whom we saw almost every day. At a given distance, we threw rocks and laughed as each one hit. We were doing this for several minutes, unaware that Mr. Baxter had come out into his yard with his shotgun. Just as another rock landed on his house, he fired into the air. At that moment, we did not throw another rock but ran to Verble's house a short distance away.

A few minutes later, Mr. Baxter came walking up to her house with his shotgun on his arm and said, "Some boys were rocking my house a few minutes ago." At that point, Flurice said to us, "So that's what you guys were doing?" Herbert manned up and confessed to Mr. Baxter that we were the ones who did it and we were very sorry. Mr. Baxter just laughed and said, "Okay. Now I'll get back and try to get some rest."

This Could Have Done Me In

There were certain signs that you were growing up based on the privileges that your parents gave you. First, you got to lead the mule. Then, you could hold the lines as the mule pulled the wagon. Eventually, you could hitch the mule to the wagon, and finally you had the chance to plow with the mule. I had graduated through all of these phases and was using Tony, our biggest mule, to drag the rows for planting.

Dragging was a fun job. After the rows had been plowed, you hitched the mule to the drag. The drag was made of broad boards with hooks at each end where they could be connected to trace line of the mule's gear. You rode the drag as the mule pulled it to smooth the rows for planting.

I was dragging with Old Tony, and Dad was running the single-row planter with Old Mike.

One of our friends, Joe Hunt, from the city of Jackson was visiting with us in the field. This was a new and exciting experience for him. Meanwhile, Old Tony loved the word "Whoa" and was always glad to stop for rest.

On this day, I was enjoying dragging of the rows. The soft ground felt good to my bare feet when I occasionally stepped off of the drag but most of the time riding suited me fine. Joe came across the field to bring me water; as he came near, he threw up his hand and said something that sounded like "Whoa" to Old Tony's ears. He stopped suddenly. When he did this, I fell up against Old Tony's rear. He lunged when this happened, leaving me in between the trace chain and the ground. As I fell, he started running with the drag. The drag ran me into the ground, creating a life-threatening situation. Thank God, his hooves missed me. It all happened so quickly, I hardly realized how close I came to being seriously injured or even killed.

By the time Tony ran to the end of the field, Dad was there to stop him and calm him down. When I excitedly explained what had happened, he did not scold me but put me right back to work. I may have thanked Joe for the water, but somehow I don't remember being thirsty anymore.

I Will Always Remember the Time I Forgot

It was my sophomore year in high school, after I had been in several plays and done speaking at church so school officials knew that I had some speaking abilities. Mrs. Davis, our English teacher and chorus director, had promised to take the chorus to the upcoming symposium in Jackson at Lane College. She assured us that there would be many choruses there and that the competition would be great. So our excitement was primarily about participation rather than the possibility of winning. She made us practice hard as time for the symposium grew near.

Then she had an idea. She called me aside and told me that I would also be competing in the oratorical competition. It came as a shock to me, but I knew better than to disagree with her.

Within the next few days, she gave me a speech and told me to memorize it. I disliked that speech from the beginning; nowhere did it arouse my passions. Somewhere in it had a list of people who made their way to the top, by writing, singing or inventing something. I memorized the speech, but never really got my heart into it.

She rehearsed with me a number of times, but she was never too excited herself about my prospects for winning. If she had said, "Let's forget about the speech," at any point this would have been great with me. But that never happened.

On the day of the symposium, we all boarded the bus for the thirty-seven mile trip to Lane College. When we arrived, there were high school students there from as far away as Memphis, ninety miles away. After a long list of choral groups singing, then came the oratorical contest.

After one or two speakers, a male student from a school in Memphis came to the stage. He spoke in a powerful, well-prepared way on Frederick Douglass. I could see the holes in my preparation, and that I had little chance of beating that speech.

Soon they called my name. Slowly, I walked to the podium and began my speech. About midway through my speech, I forgot the next line. I paused for what seemed a long moment, said, "Excuse me," and got back on track. Not feeling too good about my chances, I finished the speech and slowly walked back to my seat with polite applause.

I do not know who won the oratorical contest. I know that I did not. The Frederick Douglass speech should have won according to my thinking.

The psychological impact of forgetting my speech had a long-term emotional effect on me. It made me hesitant to trust my memory. I also made me vow to never go to the podium without being prepared. It is great to be able to trust your memory, but it is also great to have preparation if the memory fails.

I chuckle now when I think back on that day. Even though I have continued in the ministry for over fifty years and taught speech at the university level over thirty-five years, I will always remember the day that I forgot.

❈ SECTION 3 ❈
They Keep Going

Chapter 7

Rose Mary, Mighty Like a Rose

ROSIE HAD THOSE QUALITIES THAT seemed ideally suited to make her a good wife for a minister. So when James Dixson, a teenage minister, came from Jackson, Tennessee thirty miles away, the die was cast and set. By some mistake, Dorothy ended up with his picture. That was soon corrected and Rosie moved to center stage in the relationship.

When James went into the military, a constant flow of letters began between him and Rosie, and it became clear that they felt that they were meant for each other. This was fine with the family because James fit the bill from the family perspective. For Mom, he was a faithful member of the Church of Christ, a preacher even. His family was also members of the church, which connected with the younger members of our family.

James's plans were to head to the Nashville Christian Institute as soon as he left the military. This was a school headed by the nationally renowned preacher, Marshall Keeble, who had lead thousands to Christ.

With only a limited education prior to his military experience, after being enrolled at Nashville Christian Institute for a short period of time, he and Rosie were ready to get married. We all laughed about how his grades improved following his marriage. One teacher returned a paper to him with a written comment saying, "Nice work, Mrs. Dixson."

Rosie and James seemed good for each other in many ways, and personally, they were very inspiring and helpful to me. When they came home, they made me very conscious of my grammar. If I said, "They was...," or "It don't..." they jumped on it and made me correct what I had said.

We were all glad when Rosie announced that she was pregnant and waited anxiously for the new addition. But this was never to be because when James took her to the hospital where an intern attempted to deliver the baby, it died. Both of them were devastated. The healthy baby had gone full term and now it was gone. Rosie always believed that she was given medication to take her life after their failure. James had her moved to the General Hospital where Dr. Crutchfield nursed her back to health.

It was at this point that we decided to go to Nashville. My sister Verble, Mom, and I were designated to make the trip by bus. This was to be an eye-opening trip for me. The visit was helpful for Rosie, lifting her spirits and helping her heal. It was wintertime and all of us, including James' sister, bedded down in the small apartment. I had the privilege of visiting the Nashville Christian Institute and meeting Brother Marshall Keeble for the first time. I remember a group of preachers talking in chapel and remarked later, "I really liked that little guy that spoke at the end." To which my brother-in-law replied, "That was Brother Keeble." Since it was a time of their lectureship, I also had the chance of seeing other great ministers including Luke Miller, L.M. Jones and George Robbins.

After Rosie's recovery, she never was able to have children again. They took in the children of several family members and reared them as their own. James graduated from NCI and enrolled at Tennessee A & I College, later completing a Masters Degree. He became the minister of the South Hill Church of Christ in Nashville, where he served for several years. They later moved to Scottsboro, Alabama, the home of the famous Scottsboro Boys' case. After serving the church there for a period of years, he moved to Virginia where he preached for a local church and attended the state college there.

Finally, when the North Jackson, Tennessee Church of Christ decided to construct a new building and start a congregation in nearby Denmark, Tennessee, they wanted James, a hometown boy, to be the minister. He and Rosie were happy to get a fresh start near their home. The work there thrived until it was time for James to retire.

They moved into the city of Jackson, Tennessee and attended the East Jackson Church of Christ where James occasionally preached. One of my students at Southwestern Christian College, Lovell C. Hayes, is the current minister of this congregation.

Chapter 8

Pushed and Pulled

ALTHOUGH SELMER WAS NOT MUCH DIFFERENT from most southern towns its size, it was a home for me in spite of racism. I was sometimes the victim of traditional racism though I did not come face-to-face with it on a daily basis. I lived in an area with mostly black neighbors, and I went to an all black church and an all black school. There were some white people, who lived fairly close to us along the road, but we seldom went into their house and they seldom came into our house.

I appreciate the fact that our parents did their best to insulate us from confronting racism head on. They first taught us how to live a dual life; one around whites and another around blacks and especially family members. This validated the words of W.E.B. DuBois who said, "Deception is the defense of the weak." This became a survival technique for many blacks.

More specifically, our mother warned us of our behavior around white people. "Do not look them in the eye or ever touch them," was her warning. As two black psychologists pointed out, historically, black mothers psychologically emasculated their sons in order to protect them from violent reprisals.

Our father minimized our contact with white young men, close to us in age, because he knew what could happen if our games ended in a racial fight. Boys wanted to play and have fun. I remember the time that my brothers and some friends were playing baseball against a group of white boys. Dad came and ended the game, sending my brothers and their friends' home for no apparent reason. But he was wise in realizing what could happen.

I only learned recently why my mom and Dad never let any of my sisters do domestic work. My personal bias was that all of my sisters were fine looking girls. Dad and Mom knew the perils of having them working among white men who had a high rate of immoral acts with black women. They simply refused to allow the risk.

Whenever we ventured outside our comfort zone, we knew the drill of going to the balcony only when we went to a movie, being served at the "colored" window at the local Dairy Queen, going to the "colored" waiting room at the Greyhound bus station, to go to the back of the bus after being the last to board.

The church was no exception. The white Church of Christ gave us some songbooks, which made us very happy. Within a week, they came to pick them up, because they said they had made a mistake, and replaced them with some ragged books that looked just like the hand me down books we got in school each year.

After I had been preaching for a few years, I was asked to conduct a tent meeting behind the black high school in Lexington, Tennessee. It began on Sunday afternoon, and chairs had to put down before the service began. I was pleased to see the local white minister drive up, shed his coat and begin working. But that feeling was to be short lived, when he yelled to a fellow white man who came, "Get some of those nigger brothers to help put out these chairs."Katydids *had* been chirping, birds *had* been singing, mosquitoes were buzzing, right up until the moment he said that. At that moment, it was as if a broker named E.F. Hutton had something to say.

When I was leaving high school, James C. Taylor, the super-intendent of schools in McNairy County, and a member of the Church of Christ, took an interest in me. He wanted me to be the first black student to enroll at Freed-Hardeman College, which was a Church of Christ school. They wrote back after several weeks stating they had no provisions for colored students to enroll at the college. To add insult to injury, they suggested that I go to the Nashville Christian Institute. At that time, NCI was the equivalent of a high school program, and I had just graduated from high school. I never heard from James C. Taylor again.

As we finished high school, we realized sooner or later we had to leave Selmer. Since there were few jobs there, looking forward to a bright future was not a reality. Being a teacher or a preacher were the only option at the professional level, and since there were no full-time preachers of color in Selmer that only left teaching as a possibility. To be a teacher, you had to go to college, and those few positions were usually for life once individuals got into one of them.

From a laborer's perspective, you might get a low paying job at a service station, or work at a sawmill if you had the physical stamina, or otherwise find work on a farm. So we realized that if you wanted to get beyond these jobs you had to leave, sooner or later.

This was the push, but there was also the pull. People returned from up north, from places like Chicago or Detroit, with good clothes and pretty cars, making us think that they had "made it." The question for us was how we could make the transition, and the answer to that was usually a family member who had already gotten settled in a northern city. In my case, it was Vernell and Kanoa in Decatur, Illinois.

Vernell Goes to Decatur, Illinois

Vernell had moved on from Hookers Bend after High School, eventually finding her way to Union City, Tennessee, where she lived with Dad's brother, Uncle Arthur, and his wife, Aunt Mattie. There she met, and married Kanoa Browning, and the newlyweds headed for Decatur, Illinois. Kanoa had a brother who lived there who was willing to help them until they could get settled. With Kanoa's skills and his willingness to work, it did not take long for him to find work. It was not too long before Vernell also found work.

Our family had met him several times prior to their marriage. They also learned to love him for his outgoing, down-to-earth friendliness. He always had a big smile and could relate to almost anyone. The boys liked Kanoa for his interest in sports, and he even brought us a softball and gloves.

When he bought Vernell a bicycle, it really became our bicycle. All of us, except Rosie, learned to ride it, and we kept it in the family long after they were married. It was the only bike that we ever owned. So we felt good about Vernell's marriage to Kanoa and felt that he would make a good husband for her. Along the way, he also became a member of the Church of Christ.

It seemed rather easy for them to get settled in Decatur, and from Vernell's letters, it was not long before we felt that they were doing well. Vernell found the Greenwood Avenue Church of Christ, where she placed her membership and began working in the congregation. She was pleased to find that the primary family that started the congregation, and many of the members, were from Tennessee; this made her feel right at home.

As I later learned, Decatur was a working city of sixty to seventy thousand people. Many from the south were drawn to this city because they found work at the foundries, the Staley Starch Company, and the Caterpillar Company, which still produces and sells its products all over the world. There were many other opportunities with smaller operations in that city. It seemed that there was a great part of the black population from Brownville, Tennessee, near Selmer.

The black Americans who came from the south brought with them a work ethic that made them good employees. Also, leaving the southern states where there were fewer opportunities, they had a strong desire for home ownership and to have the things which many of them had been denied.

Vernell and Kanoa were models of hospitality toward other families. They became an "above ground" railroad for family members wanting to leave the south. First to come were our sister Dorothy and her husband Tee Spence.

Dorothy's married life began in Mississippi doing what she had been a part of all of her life, farming. Only this time, instead of being surrounded by brothers and sisters it was just Tee and her. It was a hard life but they were in love and they enjoyed being together.

It was not too long before she was pregnant with their first child, which was lost to a miscarriage. She sought solace from Mom, who reminded her that she was still young and could have other children.

Ollie's prediction came true because it was not too long before Dorothy was pregnant again. She was happy as the pregnancy progressed but this was also to bring disappointment when she miscarried again. Tee buried the fetus in a shoebox in their backyard.

During this time, their religious convictions sustained them. They worshipped at the Meigg Street Church of Christ in Corinth. An old minister who came from Memphis would visit the congregation and stay for weeks at their house. This became a blessing in disguise. Tee had recently become a Christian but had many questions about the church. Brother Gotral patiently took his time and answered every one of them. Thus a solid foundation was laid for a lifetime of service in the church, where Tee later became an elder. It was also helped to lay a strong spiritual foundation in the family of this newlywed couple.

Times were tough and farm work was hard, with little money to be earned. After weighing their options, they decided to move up north to Chicago where Tee had lived for a time prior to their marriage.

His aunt, Babe, lived there and at least they could stay with her for a brief time.

The Spence's Take to the Road

Chicago was thought to be a promised land of the north, along with several other major cities like Philadelphia and New York. There seemed to be an abundance of evidence to support these claims. Many who left the south for one of these cities returned with endless talk of how well they were doing. However, reality proved much of this to be untrue.

The apartment was tiny, and the kitchen and the living area had to be shared with other residents. This was strange and difficult for Dorothy. The kitchen could only be used at a certain time and it had to be cleaned when you finished. This became a friction point because all users did not always cooperate. Sometimes Dorothy was blamed for the negligence of others, who used the cooking area after her and left it unclean. Inviting guests from the church or other friends was out of the question.

Tee found a job at the Campbell Soup Company. Although he handled the work assignments, he had another problem. As a T.B. victim in early childhood, he was left with a speech impediment that made it difficult for him to enunciate his words. Nearly all the workers around him were white immigrants from Poland or Germany. They understood each other, but they could not understand Tee, and he could not understand them. One could imagine the difficulty in working in such an environment eight hours per day, forty hours per week. Tee simply did not like it. Plus, you had no time to leave work to look for another job.

Dorothy found work at a mattress factory, but she experienced problems too. Having worked hard all of her life, she quickly adjusted to the sewing tasks. Her problem was getting to and from work. They had no car and she had to ride the 'L' train for quite a distance. Being unfamiliar with Chicago, this presented a huge challenge for her; she dreaded going to work and returning home due to having to ride that train. Although they had some money both of them were experiencing urban stress.

The major joy that they experienced was attending the Michigan Avenue Church of Christ. There were many members, along with the minister and associate minister, who were also from Tennessee. They enjoyed the friendly atmosphere, the worship style and the sermons from the pulpit. There was little the Church could do to alleviate their work and living conditions, although it did help them to deal with some of the stress.

Beginning to realize that being "Up North" was not all that it was supposed to be, they began to share with each other their stresses and how their expectations were not being realized. Finally they both agreed and said, "Let's go home." And that was exactly what they did. Once back in Mississippi, they found life to still be tough and the work hard, but much more relaxing. It felt good to be back home among friends and family and church members. Dorothy became pregnant again, and on September 29, 1949, she delivered her first child, a baby boy. They named him Howard Tee Devon Spence. There was much joy in the Bowers and the Spence families. Again, they settled down to live a hard but "good" life. Dorothy had her baby, her flowers, her garden and her Christian husband.

On the Road Once More

Dorothy and Vernell were always close. I remember when Vernell visited from Decatur and Dorothy came to Selmer from Corinth to visit us. We had a good time, but Dorothy and Vernell spent a considerable time off to themselves talking. Later, I learned that they were exploring the possibility of Dorothy and Tee moving to Decatur. As Howard reached his first birthday, this became a reality, but this time with more preparation than their experiment in Chicago.

Vernell had already arranged for them to live with a faithful Christian family, the Dismukes. They placed their membership with the Greenwood Avenue Church of Christ where they met more members of the Church who had come from Tennessee.

Tee found a job at Wagner's Malleable Iron Company while Dorothy settled down to become a full-time wife and mother. She felt comfortable under the watchful eye of her big sister and her newfound Christian friends. This eventually led to six more children, all born in Decatur, and them becoming members of Greenwood Avenue Church of Christ, which later became the Jasper Street Church of Christ.

Major later followed the same path, making a home in Decatur. For a while, Verble and Flurice do the same, but only briefly, before returning to Tennessee.

Chapter 9

On My Journey Now

AFTER SPENDING TWO SUMMER MONTHS "up north" in Decatur and then returning to Tennessee to speak in two week-long revivals, it was time for me to head back to Illinois. By this time I had gained a little traction towards my "true north" direction. Going back to Decatur, where I had already pre-enrolled at Millikin University, and preached several sermons at the Greenwood Avenue Church of Christ, I had made a number of Christian friends, all making things a little easier for me.

Again I boarded a Trailways bus in Selmer, across from the Ritz Theater, with a sense of certainty and about five-hundred dollars in my pocket, from the two revivals and personal gifts. The ride did not seem as long as the first one, and when we stopped in Saint Louis, I got up the nerve to wander through the bus station during the one-hour wait for the Decatur bus.

Once back in Decatur, it was actually time for me to enroll at Millikin. I was a week late in signing up for classes and had missed all of the freshman orientation programs and the first class meetings. Fortunately, I was sent to a kind professor who was to become my mentor and one of my best friends while I was at Millikin. Dr. Raymond Brewer was a kind man with a soft voice and he actually cared for students. He managed to get me enrolled in classes. I was surprised, as we walked through the halls, that I only saw maybe four black male students and no black female students. The next day, I attended my first class wearing the traditional white and blue cap, with the traditional short bill. This was the beginning of my frustration. Being a week late, I had to take what was left of the course selection. These were classes at the most inconvenient times, and in most cases with the least popular professors. Almost every class required a great deal of reading. They included, freshman English, Biology, Western civilization, and New Testament Studies. Dr. Brewer talked me out of taking Greek, which he thought ministers should have taken in their last two years of college, to prepare them for seminary. Not being a Catholic, I wanted to ask, *"What is seminary?"* but I figured I would find out later. I thanked him for postponing Greek when I finally took it in my last two years at Millikin, as he had advised.

The only friendly face that I saw in my new classes was the one of Dr. Brewer who taught the New Testament class. In my first year in college, I was taking several heavy reading classes, a lab class, biology; all while being introduced to a strange and new social environment.

It seemed that the only security blanket that we had in classes was that freshmen beanie, that short-billed cap, which all freshmen were told we had to wear everywhere. Then I remember, my English teacher, Dr. Neal Doubleday, finally saying one day, "Take off those silly caps."

After having been a top student at a segregated and isolated school, now I was struggling in every class in college. Trying to survive, I sat between two very bright students, Janet Bowman on one side and Jim Ballowe on the other. Neither paid much attention to me, and they weren't very friendly. Rushing from my 8 a.m. P.E. class without having had breakfast, I had to turn and squirm many times in my seat as my stomach began to growl.

It seemed that I was almost programmed to fail and, possibly some may have been surprised to see me back for my second year. At the end of the first year, my grade point average was 1.6, and I was on academic probation.

I had to work during that first year. Early in the year I saw an ad in the paper offering work for Millikin University students and, since I was one, I went to apply. I got the job, but not the best hours. It was four hours for four days per week, from 11 p.m. to 4 a.m. Just when it was time to go to sleep, it was time to go to work. I was the only black guy on the job, and there were some nice co-workers, but some were overtly racist. Because I was from Tennessee, "Estes Kefauner," a Tennessee politician, became my nickname. Even the supervisors called me that; I let them know I did not appreciate it, but I refused to let it bother me.

I often wondered how I survived that first year in college. I have concluded that it must have come from three positive sources: my family, church members, and the words of my high school principal at my graduation. Professor Ledbetter said on that occasion, "There is not a student anywhere north, south, east, or west, better than Calvin Bowers." I could not let him down.

I have thought about that statement often, especially when I got papers returned with a 69 or 70. I had to realize that Professor Ledbetter was only expressing his opinion. What was the extent of his experience in a small all black school in a city of 5,000 total citizens? I learned one truth from this statement— speak of people in terms of what they can become, and if they believe it, they will work hard to prove you right.

Several times I have spoken to Professor Ledbetter and asked him to release me from the things he said about me. Each time we had a good laugh and talked about the old school days. I learned so much from this man.

A humbled, harder working sophomore reentering school in the fall of 1952, I knew that I had to do better, but I was not exactly sure how. A timely blessing occurred in the schedule of my fall classes. I was enrolled in an Old Testament class taught by the Devotional Dean, Emerson I. Abendroth, who we called "Abbey." He was a kindly man who spoke in a soft voice. I will never forget his saying when he returned the midterm tests, of all the fifty people in this class the highest grade made in this test was 91, and there were three in the class. I never knew who the other two were but when I received my paper, I prayed a silent prayer and thought, "Maybe I do belong."

About that time, my brother-in-law took me to Wagner's Malleable Iron Company where he and my other brother-in-law, Tee Spence worked. The hiring foreman took one look at me and realized a problem was my weight, which was only 130 pounds.

He said, "I thought you told me that this man was heavier than this." Kanoa had a quick reply as he expected questions and said, "Yes, but he is a hard worker." That must have worked because the foreman told me to come to work the next day.

I will never forget my first night at Wagner's. The noise was so loud that you had to shout into a person's ear to talk to them. I did not see how I could take this for eight hours, but the worst was yet to come.

The foreman took me upstairs and introduced me to the men who were already working; one was called "Big Man." The foreman gave me a pair of pads for my hands and told Big Man what I would be doing. The job of catching castings on the conveyors was so hot that we worked one hour and took a thirty-minute break. I made it the first night and about three more days with Big Man's crew. Then, I was moved downstairs onto the casting table. This job was much easier and much cooler, and I worked hard to support what Kanoa had said. On Friday, I had a great feeling when I received a paycheck of almost $100. I was doing a man's job and getting a man's pay.

Chapter 10

Jewell Irene: Following In Our Footsteps, Following Her Own Dreams

AFTER A YEAR AT A & I STATE University in Nashville, Tennessee, our parents would not allow Jewell to go to New York to earn the tuition money she needed to re-enter school in the fall. She fondly remembers that she liked music, art, and dancing, but the dancing had promptly ended at the time of her baptism, on Mom's orders.

During that year of college, she had met Harold Trice, Jr. from Henderson, Tennessee, and they had begun to talk of marriage. Harold had been in the military and was a faithful member of the Church of Christ, but he still had to pass a test tougher than any from his military experience; he had to ask Mom and Dad's permission. He started with Dad, the easier of the two, who responded, "I don't know..., I guess..., I reckon it might be sort of fine, if she wants to go." Jewell remembers, Mom just flat out told him, "I have five daughters and I didn't have one to give away. She is grown though, and if she wants to go she may."

"I went," Jewell said, "we were married on November 11, 1956, and we are still happy with each other." They started their family by living in a small house in Jack's Creek, Tennessee. Soon thereafter they went to Decatur, Illinois seeking employment. After about six months, they returned to Henderson.

Herbert Hoover: The Traveling Man

I asked Herbert what best described his role as he related to the family. He thought for a moment and replied, "The Traveling Man, would be just fine." Not only did he spend over twenty years in the Air Force, but also he was traveling before he went into the military.

His first venture away from home began when he met our cousin, Elbert Bowers, at the county fair in Jackson, Tennessee. Elbert had a photo stand, where people could have a picture taken, and it would be ready for them within minutes; quite a novelty in those days. Elbert talked to Herbert and asked him to go on the road with him to join another worker named Willie. Having just graduated from high school, and with no job, Herbert agreed to do it. He enjoyed traveling from city to city in various states, meeting new people, especially girls. In spite of having lots of fun, the low pay told Herbert that he would soon need to move on.

Back in Selmer, with the help of our old school teacher, Laurthree Westbrook, he filled out the application papers for A & I State University. He was notified two weeks later that he was accepted. Leaving for Nashville with a friend, Leonard Moore, who had just gotten out of the Army, Herbert arrived at the single bedroom apartment of Rosie and James after a two and half-hour ride. His work in Selmer at Boggins Lumber Yard, and some construction work, had not earned him enough money to buy a suitcase, so he took his clothes in a cardboard box. Although Rosie and James welcomed him, he soon learned that three was a crowd and it would be time for him to move on.

Fortunately, James introduced him to Frank Thorpe, who eventually became like a father to him. Frank and his wife offered Herbert and Kelly Mitchell, a preaching student at Fisk University, a room for thirty dollars a month. Herbert settled in on the lower bunk. When James began receiving his GI allotment, he introduced Herbert to two jobs that he was leaving. One was as a dishwasher at the V.A., and the other was working weekends for a rich family in West Nashville. Herbert soon learned to ride the bus to work and began to feel comfortable on those jobs. A short while later, Frank offered him a paper route, for which he had get up at 4 a.m., but it was a chance to make more money.

As Herbert settled into these jobs, he began seeking to have his social needs met. He met one girl only to learn that she had a nine-month-old baby. After one date, the relationship ended, but this gave him a chance to begin to learn "the ropes." As the year progressed, Frank took an even greater interest in him as his mentor. He manipulated the paper routes and assignments to give Herbert a way to make more money.

Things were getting better. Through Frank's moves, Herbert soon had a lawyer's ten-year-old son working for him, along with the use of his dad's car to help deliver papers. He was all settled in Nashville, and thought things couldn't get any better. He was unaware of the drastic change that was on its way.

Uncle Sam Comes Calling

Around July 1951, Herbert received notice from the Selmer Local Board to report for induction into the army. While he was waiting for his paperwork to come from Nashville to Selmer, he saw a sign inviting that said, "Join the Air Force Now!" He walked in and signed up on the spot.

In a few days, he was on his way to Memphis, then on to San Antonio, Texas for basic training, then to Cheyenne, Wyoming to teletype school where they were taught how to send and receive messages. Following this training, Herbert found that his next stop would be Korea, and by this time he had earned his third stripe. This was just the beginning for the "Traveler Man." After tours in Korea, he was sent back to the States, to Panama City, Florida, where he was enrolled in NCO Academy Leadership School. It was there that he met his future wife, Tiny Wilson, and they were married on April 9, 1955. Their first child, Herbert Jr., was born the following year. Then he was assigned to Newfoundland, where Tiny and Herbert, Jr. joined him eighteen months later. A second son, Richard, was born on March 15, 1959.

After two years in Newfoundland, it was time for Herbert and Tiny, and their two children to head back to the States. They made this long trek by car, ending up in Savannah, Georgia. On May 31, 1962, Bonita was born and after moving the mother and three children into the home of Tiny's sister, her husband Herbert was off to Greenland for a year without his family. When he returned to Tampa in 1963, he bought a house in Progress Village, with a little lake in the back where he often fished at night.

Once again, this was not to last long, because just as things were about to balance out, Herbert was ordered to the Philippines. He liked his job there, but again he was taken away from his family. All the time his marriage was disintegrating. It finally got to a point where Tiny refused to come with him, although he could now afford better living conditions; the marriage ended in divorce, and all parties, including the children, suffered.

As I read this account, tears come to my eyes. Along with the rest of our family, I was ignorant of what Herbert and Tiny were going through, and the extreme pain that must have been in their lives and the lives of their children. We had no idea of the trauma. Without placing blame, people can be put in places, like the military, which put extreme pressures on family life.

I was glad to see Herbert put his life back together as well as he did. He continued to serve in the Air Force until his retirement, and he has remarried. I have visited him twice since he retired, at his home in Des Moines, Iowa. That first visit, he seemed content working at the V.A. and doing what he liked. JoAnn seemed to be a fine woman of integrity, who is easy to love. At that time, he still had some of his old habits and had not come back to the church.

Visiting him again in 2010, I was even more impressed to see him in church, working in the food pantry and doing whatever he was asked to do. JoAnn is a superb hostess and a wonderful person with whom to talk. We visited Major and his family in Decatur, and talked about the old times. While we were in

Decatur, we also spent time with our much beloved brother-in-law, Johnny Ross. When Barbara and I got married five years after the death of Mozell, my wife of forty-seven years, Herbert was there as my best man. We talk weekly and I always wish him the absolute best. The wounds have healed, but some scars remain.

I see now why he thought of himself as the traveling man, though he will not go near a plane.

Preaching, Going to School and Working at Wagner's

As I settled into my second year of college, I began to feel a need for a car. Listening to car commercials, there was one that struck me as making sense. "Come to Chicago and take over the payment of a repossessed car at a fraction of the cost," then he gave the address: 5651 Michigan Avenue, and ended by saying, "Come on in today!" I tried to think of how I could get to Chicago, two-hundred miles away. Then it hit me: Tee Spence used to live in Chicago and he knew the city.

After few days, Tee and I were on a train heading for Chicago. We took Kanoa along, just for good measure. Arriving, we went straight to the address on Michigan Avenue, and to our surprise, there was no car dealer there. We set out on foot to find a car dealer in the area that had a deal like the one I'd heard on the radio, but one was not to be found. We should have turned around and caught the train back to Decatur, but we felt that we had to find a car. At one of the dealerships, a 1948 Studebaker Starlight coupe caught my eye, so we waited for the salesman to return. After a short ride around the block I gave the man my $300 and Tee cosigned for the $500 balance.

On our way back to Decatur, the car began smoking and we had to drive very slowly to make it home. After that trip, I never liked that car again. The extra money that I had to pay, just to make it functional, was a lesson I never forgot. After driving it back to Tennessee to show it to my girlfriend and family there, I started planning to get rid of it as soon as it was paid for. I was teased quite a bit about being a pushover at the dealership. Major laughed at me, and scolded me for not buying a Chevrolet, but in the end, he helped me make the payments.

In Decatur, I was settling in as a regular preacher at the Greenwood Avenue Church of Christ. I was invited to preach at a church in Champaign-Urbana, fifty miles away, on alternate Sundays, without any type of pre-agreement of salary or other benefits, which were not really important to me at the time. As I recall, I was never given more than twenty dollars at either congregation on any Sunday for as long as I was with them.

I met really fine people and had wonderful times at both places. In Decatur, I remember the Bartons, the Greenes, the Pooles, the Cruzes, the Browns, the Dismukes, and my own family members the Spences, the Brownings, the Rosses, and the Bowers.

In Champaign-Urbana, among the most faithful members were the Andersons, Hensleys, the Kerseys, the Bellamys, and a few other families. This group met in a funeral home, but our services were not dead. I will never forget their leader, Brother Norman Anderson, who was a great source of encouragement to me. I got to know the members well because, not having any family in town, I had fewer choices for Sunday dinners. If I did not eat at the Andersons, I ate at the Hensleys, the Hersheys, or the Bellamys.

Sometimes driving back and forth from Decatur became trying, and one night, as I was returning to Decatur, I dozed off at the wheel. When I snapped awake, I was across the white line and the oncoming car was off on the shoulder to his right. He turned around, caught up to me and pulled me over using his spotlight. When he asked what happened I noticed that he was wearing an Air Force uniform and most likely from nearby Chanute Air Force Base. When I told what happened he said, "I thought that maybe you were drunk and I'd try to get you off the road." I realized then how I could have easily lost my life.

I preached for both of those small congregations until 1955. There is no way I would trade those experiences now.

During this time, I was still pursuing my studies at Millikin University. Although I was not at the top of my class, I was surviving and on my way to graduation. Although I had become more comfortable in school, courses were becoming more challenging. Subjects, such as Greek, Inductive Logic, and Experimental Psychology were hard. In addition, I had fewer people to study with and less time to study due to my work schedule. At one point, I was studying Greek and French, advanced Philosophy, and a course in Shakespeare taught by the famed Dr. Ruth Maxwell.

At Wagner's by this time, I had become a member of the Safety Committee, and had worked my way up to a Scrap Classifier. I learned all the angles and the job was relatively easy. The working hours of 3 p.m. to 11 p.m. wiped out my social life and greatly reduced my time for study.

The years of 1954 and 1955 were filled with expectations. In 1953, I saved money and made a down payment on a 1953 Chevrolet 210. It was nothing like the 1953 Impala Major had.

My car did not even have radio, but it was new. The next year I got to know Johnny Ross, who became my lifetime friend and later my brother-in-law.

Johnny rode with me back from Henderson, Tennessee on his way to Indianapolis where he had a job waiting. We persuaded him to stay in Decatur where, he got a job at the Orlando Hotel, and he later he worked at Wagner's.

Major, Johnny, and I lived together in a one-room house behind Vernell and Kanoa's house. It was cold at times, but we got along fine and had lots of fun.

When I was laid off from Wagner's from December to August, I applied through Millikin to go to a Mexican reservation on a friend's scholarship. To my surprise, I was accepted. Just when I was preparing to go, I got into a car accident and that cancelled the trip. If I'd been able to go, Herbert had agreed to make my car payments for the summer.

Its amazing how single acts and statements stick in your mind. I remember the article about the accident in the next day's newspaper mentioning that a 22-year old man was driving the car. That got my attention because it was the first time I remember being called a "man" outside of my immediate circle.

Chapter 11

Ollie's Kids, Another Generation

IT WAS NOT UNCOMMON IN THAT time to find men working two jobs. Soon Kanoa found himself falling into this. His electrician business grew and he also worked 3 p.m. to 11 p.m. at Wagner's. Vernell also found work after their two children were old enough to be left with others or to enroll in school.

Rolland Kaye Browning was the oldest, born September 8, 1953. A few years later, Gloria Jean was born. Rolland was a healthy baby and grew up to be a strong, healthy man. Very early in life, Gloria Jean began suffering health issues that continued to plague all of her life. As a very young child, she had eczema, causing itching that kept her and her mother up nights. Vernell, her mother, exhausted every possibility that she thought might help her daughter's health. With the help of her mother and other family members, Gloria moved through high school, later through college, and finally earned a Masters Degree.

She was later married to Marcus Thomas, but due to health issues and other differences, this marriage was brief. Later she had at least one kidney transplant before finally succumbing to death at the age of forty-two. She left a legacy of determination and a strong will to survive.

As the first grandchild of Henry and Ollie, Rolland received great attention from all family members. He was a handsome little boy. When Vernell brought him home to Tennessee, all of the family members were excited. This became a pattern on annual visits. He developed a special love for his grandparents in Tennessee, and going down south became a lasting infatuation with him, which extended beyond their death.

In October 1957, Jewell and Harold's first child, Ricky Benard, was born in Chester County, where their next four children were also born there. On September 4, 1959, Jerome Wendell arrived on the scene. The only daughter, Sylvia Travell, was born July 3, 1962. The third son, Billy "Joe" Jonathon, was born July 23, 1964, and their last child, John Christopher, arrived December 24, 1968.

Jewell and Harold worked hard at trying to support their family. They worked as farmers for the first twenty-five years of their marriage. They had a number of good crops, and even bought a house and a number of acres during this time. They had tractors and other quality equipment. As the boys grew up, they also were hard workers and a great help to the family. It was during this time that they helped me to purchase a small farm in Tennessee, mainly so my first wife would have a place to return to, in case something happened to me.

I recall visiting them at their farmhouse and seeing the variety of vegetables that they grew. Their children were growing up and doing well in school. Rickey was the first to go to the local Freed-Hardeman College. A few years later, Jerome graduated from high school and went to another college in Tennessee.

During this time, they grew fine crops but earned less money. Both Jewell and Harold found it necessary to supplement their income with other employment. Harold became a school bus driver for fourteen years. Jewell began working as a teacher's aide for the 6th grade class at Henderson Elementary School.

As the children grew up and began to move away, it became clearer that continuing to farm was not a viable option. In 1985, they sold the farm, and the equipment, and moved to Nashville.

Harold's first job in Nashville was as a custodian for the Schrader Lane Church of Christ. This seemed like a natural fit since they knew the minister, David Jones, and some of their relatives were members in the congregation. He remained on this job for about four years. In the meantime, Jewell worked as a librarian's assistant at the Glen Cliff High School. Harold next went to work as a custodian at the American Baptist College. Jewell was a hired as secretary at the East Middle School of Nashville.

Two years after Howard was born, Tee and Dorothy's second child, Ollie Inez Spence, came into this world, on November 7, 1951. My mother was extremely pleased for having a grand-daughter born on her birthday and also named Ollie. Next on the scene was Judy Elaine, born May 4, 1954, then Charles Edwards, the second son born on October 5, 1956. On October 29, 1959, JoAnne was born, on my dad's birthday. When discussing names for her, Henry said, "Anything but Henrietta." Her father wanted her named JoAnne, after a kind, caring woman he'd seen on a TV soap opera. The last two girls were Dorothy Nell, born on October 6, 1959, who was named after her mother and her aunt Vernell, and Marsha Faye born August 26, 1961. One more boy, Joseph, was born, but only lived for a few hours. The doctor warned Dorothy not to have any more children.

The common characteristics that Dorothy and Tee instilled into their children were loyalty to Christ and his Church, hard work, and to gain as much education as possible.

Howard, the oldest, set the bar for the rest of his siblings, and he set it high. Beginning as a very bright child in grade school, by the time he reached middle school, it was apparent that he was special. He became the first black class president as a junior in high school; then he became the valedictorian of a graduating class of several hundred students. Later that same year, 1967, he became the first Presidential Scholar from the state of Illinois. That same year he went to the White House for a reception of Presidential Scholars from across the country. He and his parents had a chance to meet President Lyndon B. Johnson in person.

In the fall of 1967, he enrolled at Michigan State University in Lansing, Michigan where he earned a Bachelor's Degree before moving to the University of Michigan and earning a law degree. He worked for the state of Michigan as an attorney in the field of labor and the prison system. He has taught at the law school of the University of Michigan, as well as the University of Phoenix. He later became a state judge in Michigan for a number of years, before retiring to maintain his own law practice and to serve as an arbitrator, in a number of states, for many organizations.

Howard set the bar high, but Ollie was ready for the challenge. Ollie Mae and Ollie Inez formed a natural bond, which lasted until my mother's death. While researching materials for this book, Ollie Inez was a very helpful resource, sharing things with me that neither I nor anyone else knew.

I remember her as a beautiful brown baby, the first girl in the family, and the Spence's first to be born in Decatur. She had to fight for her identity. She remembers that because she was a girl, expectations were not very high for her. Fortunately, she did not buy into that perception nor allow it to limit her self-esteem.

In addition to being successful in her studies in high school, her extracurricular activities included being in the Spanish and the forensics clubs, and playing the clarinet in the school band. After graduation from high school, she enrolled at the University of Illinois at Champaign-Urbana where she majored in Spanish and Latin. Later she earned a Masters in counseling from Illinois State in Bloomington-Normal. Her education finally concluded when she earned her Ph.D. from Berne University, an international graduate school.

Along the way Ollie Inez had many jobs. After graduation from college she worked in a factory for a year, as a middle school counselor, and later became an accelerated K-12 academy counselor. She also taught Spanish at a community college, and coached girl's high school track for five years.

In 1988, Ollie Inez married Jerry Taylor of Decatur, and their one child, Persephone Camille Taylor, was born May 11, 1990. Since her retirement in 2010, she attends conferences, mostly on counseling and diversity, as a presenter, while enjoying her church and community work.

The Spences' second daughter, Judy, was a friendly outgoing little girl who liked school, especially science. She graduated from high school and enrolled at University of Illinois, majoring in horticulture, and later earned a Masters Degree from Eastern Illinois College in science. She also earned a Bachelor's Degree in education, which enhanced her employment as a teacher.

While she lived in Cincinnati, Ohio she became a professional landscaper working at the Procter and Gamble Company. She won a number of awards in this profession.

After ending a failed marriage, she returned to Decatur with her two daughters, Clarinda, now a nurse in Temple, Texas, and Andrea, now a student in Arlington, Texas. For many years now, Judy has been a science teacher at McArthur High School in Decatur. Judy is a keeper of secrets, concerned about others, and willing to take on family problems. She likes perfection, and is the kind of person that many would enjoy knowing.

Charles Edward Spence was born about a month after I arrived in Los Angeles. Being extremely light-skinned, I remember his father Tee Spence telling us that people would say, "Here comes Sister Spence with that white baby." He would just laugh. From all reports, Charles was a very friendly and happy baby.

He liked to talk and make people laugh and it became apparent early on that he liked to be the life of the party. His dad once said he would frequently have a group of students around him listening, even on the playground. Occasionally, he would call me and begin by saying, "How is my favorite uncle?" As a child, Charles liked to take things apart and put them together again. He liked all kinds of music and became a fairly good piano player. He sang with the Spence family at church fellowships, and eventually became the solo artist for a quartet that he put together. He liked sports and became very good in track, and he received a scholarship in this sport from the Lincoln Land Community College in Springfield, Illinois, and traveled with the team to several states.

Charles, after a second marriage, built a spacious home for his blended family. He was able to do this because of his many years of employment as a machinist at the Mueller plant in Decatur. In recent years, Charles has had a number of problems with health issues. He perseveres with a healthy faith and a strong determination.

JoAnne was reading at the fourth grade level at four years of age but somehow became discouraged because she was held back and not allowed to enroll in school. This may have affected her reaching her full potential later.

She chose to enter the work world after high school and to get married early. Eventually she had two children, Jason and Crystal. Later, Crystal gave birth to her first granddaughter. After working on a number of jobs, she settled in Decatur, where she lives with her pit bulls. If you visited her house, and you succeeded in getting past the dogs, you would discover a beautiful array of antiques, which she has collected over the years. One would likely be welcomed with a bright smile and a cheerful voice.

Dorothy Nell's name was obviously a combination of Dorothy and Vernell, always the closest of my sisters. By the time she came along the Spence children were already known as high achievers, so it was no surprise that Dorothy Nell breezed through high school and ended up at the University of Illinois at Champaign-Urbana. She graduated with a degree in leisure studies only to find that there were no jobs available in the field. Through further studies, she got a job teaching in special education at Eisenhower High School. Actually, she has taken on a second job to help the family. Her husband, Terry Hinds, runs a barbeque pit and insists that his barbeque is the best.

They have two sons, Telli Hinds, an excellent violinist who also plays the saxophone, and loves Black History studies; Harrison, the younger son also plays the violin and loves to perform. He attends a magnet school where he is a good student athlete.

Dorothy, along with her husband, stays busy keeping up with performances, athletic games, and church activities. She is regarded as a true servant.

Ollie Inez describes her youngest sister as a brown skinned, outspoken young lady. She was bothered by the race situation in America, but she was always loyal to the Church. She was in youth programs and loved to sing. She also attended the University of Illinois and majored in accounting.

Marsha and her husband had two daughters, Ashley Inez who is planning to be married, and Breeana, the youngest, who is almost six feet tall and loves computers.

Chapter 12

Graduation and Heading for California

BY THE FALL OF 1954, I had begun to think seriously of what I might do beyond graduation. I knew that I wanted to go on in school. There was also the possibility that I might get called to military service, and I had developed a relationship with a special young lady by the name of Mozell Trice from Henderson, Tennessee.

I made the rounds of applying to the same schools associated with the Church of Christ, which had all rejected me in 1951. Their status was still the same, politely saying, "We have no provision for colored students." However, this time I included Pepperdine College in Los Angeles, which was also associated with the Church of Christ. To my surprise, a few weeks later I received a letter, from Hubert Derrick Speech, Professor and Associate Minister at the Vermont Avenue Church of Christ, stating that not only was I accepted to enroll at Pepperdine in a Masters program, but a personal note stating that they would welcome me as a member at the Vermont Avenue Church. This made me feel very good and wanted. There was just one hitch: because of my past work schedule, my GPA was only 2.2. I had to enroll as an unclassified student, but I felt confident that I could change that status soon.

What I thought was good news others were not so happy about. Family members began saying things like, "You have a good job, here. Don't be in such a hurry." Church people said things like, "You are a good preacher now, what more can you do than preach the gospel?" One man at Wagner's said, "There ain't no work out there. I have a friend who just came back from L.A." Mozell said nothing to discourage me, but I could see in her body language that she was hurt and hated to see me go so far away. Later, after we were married, she told me that she thought, at the time, that my going away might just be the end of our relationship.

I managed to learn a few other lessons as I approached my time to leave. There was a man at work called "Crow." We had the same job but on different shifts, so we talked quite a bit. I casually mentioned to him that I might be leaving, and the next day the foreman came and asked me, "Are you planning on leaving us?" When I approached Crow he said, "I told him because I didn't think you would mind." The lesson was learned from tuition paid.

A prominent white minister told me that Pepperdine would funnel a lot of information through your head, but you won't learn very much. My close friend, Johnny Ross, told me, "Cal, I have a job and if you get out there and want to come back you can get my last dime." That was a real boost, which I never forgot.

As Labor Day of 1955 approached, my plans were to spend the weekend in Tennessee with family and friends, then head for Los Angeles the day after. That weekend went all too fast. On Tuesday, September 6th at around 9 a.m., I left Selmer, on my way to California, with $900 in the trunk of my car. My parents could give me no money and I knew that. Dad gave me a shaving mug as I left, which I still have, and as I packed the trunk of my car he threw in a pair of wire-pliers, which I kept for a long time.

I left Selmer on highway 64 to Memphis and made it to Oklahoma City before dark. I tried to call a preacher there that I knew, but I wasn't able to reach him. I ended up staying in a black hotel over a black-owned drug store.

The next morning, Wednesday, September 7th, I pulled on to the famed Route 66, which I was to ride all the way to Los Angeles. I clearly remember going through Amarillo, Texas after I faintly remember going through Clinton, Oklahoma. There was no way I could know then that Clinton would be the place where I'd find my second wife, Barbara Hayes, after Mozell passed away.

I spent the second night of my trip in Albuquerque, New Mexico at a small private-owned hotel. The next morning when I got up to leave, the manager was not happy, because I woke him up even though I'd already paid him.

The third day, I experienced how hot the desert could be, with plenty of signs along the way to warn me such as, "Next Gas 100 Miles," "Last Chance to Fill Up." Since I did not have a radio, I picked up a black youth along the way and let him ride to his destination. I traveled on, spending the night in one of the hottest spots in the nation, Needles, California. The good news was that Los Angeles was just two-hundred and seventy-five miles away.

As I continued my journey on Friday morning, September 9th, I saw something I'd never seen before: groves of orange trees along the road. Hours later, I found my way to Pepperdine College, at 79th Street and Vermont Avenue, and I parked across the street on Vermont Avenue, in front of a bowling alley. I got out and walked through the doors of Pepperdine College where this part of my journey ended, and another was to begin.

Time

I remember when my grandfather died. I was thirteen and missed walking by as he sat in his swing under the big oak tree on my way to Verble and Flurice's house. We spoke no matter how many times a day we passed by. Friends from the city laughed at us and hardly understood us when we said, "How are you by now, Grandpa?" He'd answer with one word, "Tolerable."

When he died, I missed his coming to our house, talking to my dad and telling us stories from his life. He was a great storyteller, and I never grew tired of hearing his stories, not even the one I'd heard a hundred times. I often thought that everyone should have a grandfather like that.

I knew something was wrong when I could see that his legs were swelling. When he finally passed, I recall my grandmother, Martha, saying over and over, "I just have to realize, I just have to realize." I have thought of that many times when I'm hurting from the loss of someone.

Grandmother Martha moved in with us, and when she passed away years later, I was living in California, but it just so happened that I was in Tennessee at the time. As I attended her funeral, I remembered how she had always, persistently, called me "Harrison."I thought of those little paper bags that she would always give us and say, "Take these for yourself," or, "Take these to your mother and say nothing about them to your grandpa." Those bags were always tied closed in the same way with the same message, this is something good to eat, peanuts, popcorn, or chestnuts. Whatever it was, it was her way of saying I love you.

I loved you grandma; you were always good. You were never mean in spite of Grandpa's harsh words at times. I have often wished we understood you better at that time.

We just have to realize – we just have to realize as you did.

✳ PICTORIAL SECTION ✳

My paternal grandfather, William Verdell Bowers, after whom my oldest brother was named. My grandfather died at the age of 75.

My paternal grandmother Martha Jane Bowers. She died in the early 1960's.

My father Henry Harrison Bowers at the Selmer annual carnival in his mid 40's

Henry in his early 50's

Henry in his 70's.

Ollie in her 70's.

My mother Ollie Mae Ella Ray-Bowers in front of her home church Cypress Creek in Selmer, TN. I also served as the minister at Cypress Creek when I was 17 years old.

Ollie - Circa 1950's

Henry and Ollie Bowers at church. July 1974.

Ollie at my sister Verble's house in her flower garden. Circa 1970's

My maternal great-aunt Anna Bell Crowder, the wife of Dave Crowder, from Chicago, Illinois. Circa 1920's

First sister and a twin Sarah Vernell Bowers-Browning. Circa 1940's

Vernell around the age of 18.

Vernell at the family home. Circa 1960's

Second child, first brother and a twin, William "Bill" Verdell Bowers' graduation from high school at age 18.

Twins William Verdell and Sarah Vernell Bowers-Browning. Circa 1950's

Verdell Bowers - Circa 1980's

Third child and second sister Verble Mae Bowers-Atkins. Circa 1950's

Verble and husband Flurice Atkins early in their marriage. Circa 1940's

Verble at the family home. Circa 1970's

Fourth child and second brother Major Ross Bowers in his teenage years.

Major in his 20's.

Major and wife Lucille at a family wedding.
Circa 1980's -1990's

Fifth child and third sister Rose Mary
Bowers-Dixson early in high school. Circa
1940's

Rose at the Selmer annual carnival in high
school.

Rose and husband, James Dixson. The only photo taken while she was pregnant. 1947

Rose and James in their later years of marriage. Circa 1980's

Sixth child and fourth sister Dorothy Magdalene-Spence at the Selmer annual carnival.

Dorothy in high school. Circa 1940's

Dorothy and husband Tee Spence in 1983.

Seventh child and third brother Herbert Hoover
Bowers in high school. Circa 1950's

Herbert before entering the military.
Circa 1950's

Herbert in the military in his early 20's.

Herbert and wife JoAnn in 1984.

Eighth child Calvin Harrison Bowers at the age of 7 years old in 1939. I was told to pose this way because Shirley Temple posed with her hand to her cheek.

Calvin at the age of 14. I began preaching at 14 in my second hand coat worn in this photo.

Calvin in last year of high school. This is when I began wearing bow ties.

Calvin as a senior year at Millikin University. I thought glasses were the "in" thing.

Calvin in undergraduate school upon receiving a BA in Philosophy and Psychology at Millikin University in Decatur, Ill. 1955

Calvin in later years in 2000.

Jewell at the Selmer annual carnival at the age of 9.

Ninth child and fifth sister Jewell Irene Bowers-Trice at age 4 or 5.

Jewell in high school.

Jewell as a wife and mother of five children. Circa 1970's

Church building in Selmer, TN where I preached my first sermon at the age
of 14 years old.

McNairy County High School where six of my brothers and sisters and I attended.

My son-in-law Samuel Dean Bailey, daughter, Lori Bailey and
me at Ollie Lane in Henderson, TN. This road was named after
my mother at our Deerpointe Housing construction site.
Circa 2000's

Three of my siblings and brother-in-law Flurice Atkins pictured with the Hunt family from left to right, Jewell, standing far left, Herbert, back center with straw hat, Verble and Flurice standing far right. I am kneeling in the front middle. Circa 1940's

My mother and son-in-law Tee Spence standing in the front middle at the Cypress Creek Church of Christ. My father is standing to the far right. Circa 1970's

My sisters left to right, Rose, Jewell, and Dorothy. Circa 1960's

My sisters and their husbands left to right, Harold and Jewell Trice, Dorothy and Tee Spence. I am standing on the far left. Circa 1960's

Verble and me with our dad on the front porch of his home. He made the swing we are sitting in. Circa 1980's

Sitting on the front porch with my dad. I fold my arms just like him. Circa 1980's

My three brothers, Verdell, Major and Herbert in Nashville. I am standing on the far right. Circa 1990's

Six of my eight siblings left to right Verdell, Verble, Jewell, Rose, Major, and Herbert. I am standing 2nd from the right. Circa 1990's

The last picture of all my siblings together. Taken at our father's (Henry Harrison Bowers) funeral in August 1986. Left to right back row William "Bill" Verdell, Herbert Hoover, Major Ross. Left to right seated Jewell Irene, Verble Mae, Dorothy Magadalene, Sarah Vernell, and Rose Mary. I am standing in the second row at the far right.

Visiting with my brother Major in Decatur, IL.

Me and Herbert at the National Lectureship in 2005.

The last picture I took with my oldest brother Verdell and his wife Bea in Nashville, TN. May 2005

The entire junior and senior class on the front steps of McNairy County High School. Teacher Mabel B. Davis in the center holding the cake. I am standing on the far right, second from the bottom row.

Herbert on the McNairy County High School basketball team. Herbert is second from the right kneeling. 1947-1948

My graduating class at McNairy County High School. I am located on the left side in the bottom photo.

A non-fraternal independent group at Millikin University - Circa 1950's

My first friends in Los Angeles, from left to right Joe
Brasher and Carl Baccus at Clifton's Cafe in Downtown
Los Angeles. Circa 1950's

My dear friends from Tennessee and
Los Angeles, the late Katrina and Joe
Brasher.

My mentor and like my father, the late
R.N. Hogan, minister of the Figueroa
Church of Christ. Circa 1960's

R.N. Hogan on a fishing trip
in Tennessee during our
family trip together in the
70's.

My wife Barbara, and my High School English
teacher, Mabel B. Davis standing in the middle.
Summer 2007

Great gospel mentors and friends. Left to
right, the late G.S. Winston and late G.P. Holt.
They were two men whom I learned much
from. Summer 1998

My good friend and outstanding Civil Rights
attorney to Rosa Parks, and Martin Luther
King, Jr., Fred Gray. Circa 2000's

Luncheon honoring Nancy Reagan, the wife
of the late President Ronald Reagan. She is
standing fourth from the left. Circa 1990's

Standing left to right, my brother Herbert, and good friends Odra "OJ" Dyson and William "Bill" Harper at the 2005 Nashville, Lectureship.

Shaking hands with Martin Luther King III, son of the late Civil Rights leader Martin Luther King, Jr. - Circa 1990's

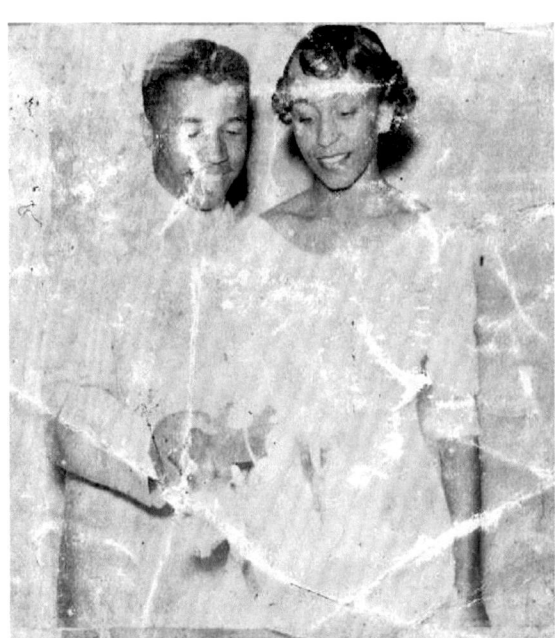

My late wife Mozell and me at our wedding reception in Los Angeles, CA in 1956. She was always a beautiful woman to me.

My wife Mozell and our three children left to right, Byron Calvin, Crystal Deneen and Lori Desta. Circa 1980's

Verble and "B" at her home on the front porch. Circa 1980's

Lori's high school graduation from Pacific Palisades. June 1995

Crystal and Lori graduating with their Master's in psychology from the Graduate School of Education and Psychology-Pepperdine University. Crystal's daughter Taylor is in the middle. May 2003

Mozell and me at the 58th Annual Pepperdine University Lectureship during a special appreciation luncheon honoring us with the Distinguished Christian Award. May 2001

Me and my lovely wife Barbara Hayes-Bowers. We were married in 2006.

...and the journey continues.

My first granddaughter by Crystal and Robert Guy, Taylor Elaine Guy, born June 29, 2002.

My second and third granddaughters by Lori and Sam Bailey, left to right Madison Mozell, born October 25, 2006 and Reagan Ella Bailey, born October 28, 2009.

❋ SECTION 4 ❋
Will the Circle be Unbroken?

Chapter 13

Settling in at Pepperdine and Meeting New Friends

I HAD REQUESTED THE SCHOOL FIND me a room with a black family nearby. They sent me to the Jones family on Harvard Boulevard. The family was very religious, though not members of the Church of Christ. The wife had attended Pepperdine and knew quite a bit about the school. They had three well-mannered children. I was assigned a room upstairs and given kitchen privileges. After driving 1,900 miles, and for three days, I had a hot meal at a soul food place around the corner, and great night's rest. The next morning, I was ready to register into my new classes at my new school.

When I reached the registration center in the library on Saturday morning, I had a feeling that I was to experience many times later, a new environment in a new place. After four years at Millikin, I was now in a school of the Church of Christ.

I am sure that, though half-scared to death with and filled with uncertainty, I managed to smile at everyone. This was reinforced when I signed up for Dr. R.C. Cannon's class on the Epistles and he said, "I'll be glad to have you in my class." I never forgot that, and he proved to be a great teacher.

To my surprise, as I was filling out my class schedule, I was about to meet "my angel." No, not a beautiful woman that swept me off my feet, but a man, who was to become my brother for life, Joe O. Brasher. This friendly young man, seemed so sure of himself, moving through the room, and speaking to people like he owned the place. He came straight to me and said, "You must be Calvin Bowers," and before I could answer he continued, "My wife told me that you were coming to Los Angeles to enroll here." I wondered what else this man knew about me. As it turned out, he had come to Los Angeles six months earlier to be in the Masters program in Religion. And we were enrolling in some of the same classes.

I call him my angel because from that day until the day he passed away, back in Tennessee, we were the best of friends. He often told people that we'd adopted each other as brothers.

As we were leaving campus that day, he said to me, "Let me take you to see the ocean," and this really gave us a chance to get to know each other. He was about eleven years older than me, having had many life experiences. He graduated from Fisk University hoping to become a doctor, served as a medic in the military, and spent many years in construction as a cement finisher. In addition, he had an excellent knowledge of barbequing, and in his own words, "the nerve of a brass monkey." In our conversation that first day, I learned that his wife was a longtime one-room schoolteacher in Henderson, Tennessee and knew Mozell's family well. At the mention of Mozell's name, he said, enthusiastically, "You know that's my cousin?"

When he decided to turn to preaching, Brother Marshall Keeble had encouraged him to come to Pepperdine. As we got back to my car, he asked, "Where are you going to church tomorrow." "Nowhere in particular," I answered. He offered, "I'm going to this little storefront church on West Adams, you want to come with me?" When I agreed he said, "I'll pick you up at nine in the morning."

This was also about to be the opening of another door in my life. When I went to the West Adams congregation, it was small and intimate, with a down-to-earth down home preacher from Texas, Jesse Walton. His wife was just as friendly as he was. There were also a number of people from Tennessee there, and some of them knew Rosie and her husband, James, who at that time preached at the South Hill Church of Christ in Nashville. After that day, I visited several other congregations, but the West Adams Church became my home base. The Townsends, the Blacks, the Browns, and the Waltons were the nucleus of the congregation.

In the following year I met Carl Baccus, Tommie Flax, Ernest Shaw, Robert McCobb, Eugene Lawton, John Whitley, Jesse Reed, Vanderbilt Lewis, Carroll Pitts, Billy English, and several others who also attended Pepperdine. We were the dreamers who tried to improve ourselves educationally and spiritually, in order to serve God.

My GPA at Pepperdine had risen to 3.7. As a ministerial student, I had avoided the military, and Mozell and I maintained a stream of letters back and forth between Tennessee and California. We talked of marriage now, with specific plans. Joe's wife, Katrina, had joined him and had moved into the house he'd purchased on West 55th Street.

Carl Baccus joined our circle of friends, and was based at the Figueroa Church of Christ, where he occasionally preached. He told Brother R.N. Hogan about me being a graduate student at Pepperdine, and a preacher, and Brother Hogan invited me to speak one Sunday night. The collection for me that night was forty-one dollars, and I felt extremely blessed. Later, during a citywide gospel meeting, a Baptist minister came into the Church of Christ and he was encouraged to attend Southwestern Christian College in Terrell, Texas. He left behind a storefront church on 103 Street in Watts. Carl was later sent by the Figueroa congregation take over the property. About that same time, Marion Holt, the Associate Minister at the Figueroa Church of Christ left to work with a church in Phoenix, Arizona. Carl must have given me a very good recommendation to Brother Hogan, because he began talking to me about the possibility of coming to the Figueroa Church of Christ as his associate preacher.

Finally, Mozell and I set the date for our wedding in November 1956. Joe's mother was coming from Henderson to L.A. for a visit, and she and Mozell came on the bus together. We were married November 21, 1956, and I began working as the assistant minister to Brother Hogan on the first Sunday in January, 1957.

Our Life at the Figueroa Church of Christ
I was in awe to be a minister at such a large church. The people were very friendly and glad to have us, but I knew my work was

cut out for me. R.N. Hogan was a progressive thinker and was open to almost every idea that I had.

I never met a man like R.N. Hogan. He had a nickname for everyone. He called me "Son," he called Mozell "Daughter," and we called him "Pops." From 1957 to his death in1995, Brother Hogan and I collaborated on the development and improvement of many successful programs at the Figueroa Church of Christ. To name a few: the Bible School, youth program, citywide meetings, Campaigns for Christ, the bus ministry, the Zone Program, Los Angeles Bible College, and missionary programs. This is not to suggest that we did all of these ourselves, because we had many associate ministers, Church leaders and members working with us. Between the years of 1961 and 2006, the following men were at one time associate ministers at the Figueroa congregation, Carroll Pitts Jr., John E. Jackson, Woodie Morrison, Curtis McCullom, Vincent Hawkins, Apollos Maxwell, and Chris Mitchell. Each made a special contribution to our work.

In 1967 when Dr. Jack Evans was selected as the new president of Southwestern Christian College, he asked me to come and serve as Academic Dean. I had known Jack for ten years by that time. That was a unique challenge for both Brother Hogan and me. We agreed that I would take a two-year leave from the Figueroa congregation to go to Southwestern, returning to Figueroa after that. Brother Hogan added a couple of stipulations. The Figueroa Church would supplement the difference in my salary, and I would return each summer to direct the Vacation Bible School.

There was no doubt the move would be a challenge. By this time, I was busy on the national scene, conducting many teacher-training sessions and revival meetings, and had just recovered from a five-week stay in the hospital, which was caused partly by exhaustion. After prayer and discussion, Mozell and I, satisfied with Brother Hogan's arrangement, were ready and willing to go.

Southwestern turned out to be a blessing in disguise for me. We enjoyed the time we spent at Southwestern as a part of the administration, teaching classes and serving as interim minister at the West End Church of Christ. One would have to be on the campus on a daily basis to fully appreciate what Dr. Jack Evans, and his staff, has done. They have made many contributions to our brotherhood and many individuals are deserving of continued support.

Those two years at Southwestern were a special blessing to me, enriching my experience and preparing me for the challenge that lay ahead back in Los Angeles.

Returning to Los Angeles and Beginning Work at Pepperdine

After the L.A. Riots of 1965, many good things were done, and many consciences were raised to a level of never being satisfied with token responses. Pepperdine, situated in what had become the heart of the city, was experiencing some new and unique challenges. Being a southern state based, rural oriented religious group, the Church of Christ has not fared as well in the city. By 1969, student groups were placing demands on the desks of college presidents. One of those demands that ended up on the desk of the Pepperdine President was for a Black Studies Program. With certain concessions, a search was underway as to who would develop and lead such a department.

Coming from the experience of the all black Southwestern Christian College validated my blackness, and my church work and associations in the Los Angeles area validated my church affiliation. Had I not been at Southwestern, I doubt if I would have been given a chance, so far as the Black Student Union was concerned. On paper I filled the bill, but still I had to accept the challenge and make it work.

Also, what was to be done about my commitment to the Figueroa Church of Christ? When I ran the proposal by R.N. Hogan, he thought it was a good idea and agreed to take it to the leaders. I will always appreciate his reply, when one of the leaders asked, "How much money is he going to be getting?" Brother Hogan explained, "That is not our business." He later told me, "As long as you do your work here, that is all that counts."University President M. Norval Young made a similar statement when he said, "We want your thinking, and your mind, to be involved at Pepperdine, and for you to take your work here seriously." I tried to sincerely meet both requests and expectations for thirty-five years.

I came to Pepperdine as the Dean of Ethnic Studies with the intention of developing quality courses that would lead to a sound degree in the area. We were able to put together an interdisciplinary degree and had several graduates. We were also able to get a course, as a general education requirement, called Ethnic Perspectives. Later, when I became Dean of Urban Studies, working with Bill Satterfield, and Dean of the School of Business, Donald Simes, we developed three new degree programs, with two Masters Degrees in Urban Planning, and Public Administration, and an undergraduate Degree in

Urban Planning. A new delivery mode was also introduced with a marathon session, every fourth weekend. These were challenging degrees requiring maturity and discipline, but they became popular and were modeled by other academic divisions.

These programs ended with the opening of the new campus in Malibu in 1972, the closure and sale of the Los Angeles campus, and my move to Malibu in 1976 as a professor of Communication and the university position of Equal Opportunity Officer. I still taught courses in the Religion and Communication division, such as The Urban Church, and Interracial Communication.

This position allowed me to work through the University to enhance minority recruitment, employment, retention and promotion. This also allowed me to have a greater role in management training with the Personnel Department, operating at the level of a full professor, and gave stability to the Equal Opportunity position.

I was able to stay up to date in the field of Equal Opportunity and Ethnic Education by annual attendance at conferences on Ethnicity in Higher Education. While in this position, I was also able in assisting a number of applicants in getting into doctoral programs at USC and Fuller Seminary.

As I came to closure of my career at Pepperdine University, it was a bittersweet departure. I had lasted through the tenure of five presidents and into the tenure of a sixth. They were Hugh Tiner, M. Norval Young, Bill Banowsky, Howard White, David Davenport, and finally Andrew K. Benton, the current President of Pepperdine University.

My Children and My Wife

God blessed Mozell and me with three lovely children. Crystal Deneen, our oldest daughter, was born May 16, 1964 and became the pride and joy of our life. My friend, Joe Brasher, and another friend Pansy Johnson went to the hospital to pick her up. They both had special affection for her as long as they lived.

Eight years later my son, whom I almost named Lloyd, was born. Mozell and I came up with another name for him, for which he is very much grateful. But, much like I grew accustomed to being called Harrison, but *only* by my grandmother, my son says I'm the only one who still calls him by his given name. To everyone else, he's just "B." He was a healthy baby and an inquisitive young boy. He had a love for animals and reading. At grade seven, he was already reading at a twelfth grade level. He had an inquisitive mind and asked questions about everything. And much like my sister Dorothy, if he wasn't satisfied with the answers, he would have more questions.

Following our one and only trip to Ethiopia in 1976, Mozell found that she was expecting another child. Church members concluded that the child was conceived in Ethiopia, though we never thought so. We left Ethiopia a few days early, to pick up Crystal and B. in Henderson, but we also wanted to spend some time with my parents.

On March 18, 1977, Mozell delivered a 4.7-pound baby girl at the Daniel-Freeman Hospital in Inglewood, California. I was privileged to name her, just as I had named B. I named her Lori, and in honor of our trip to Ethiopia the year before, we gave her the middle name, Desta, recommended by our friends the Kelbisows. Desta means "joy" in Amharic, the official language of Ethiopia.

This completed our family circle. All three of our children grew up and were baptized at the Figueroa Church of Christ, where they attended Sunday school, and participated in many youth programs as part of the Figueroa Family.

Mozell, wife and mother, was very content to be a stay-at-home mom, while I made the living for her and the children. Thanks to her, our children were never "latchkey kids."

One of our greatest joys was traveling to Henderson and Selmer each year to see our families. The children had cousins close to their ages, and they formed lifelong relationships. All three of our children also attended the 74th Street Elementary School in Los Angeles in their grade school years.

In fourth grade, Crystal was enrolled at the Inglewood Christian School, where she remained, until she graduated from elementary school. Then she was enrolled at the Brethren High School in Paramount, which was also attended by her childhood friend from the Figueroa Church, the late Gary Beverly. During her last two years of high school, she transferred to Westchester High where she participated in several musical plays, and became President of the Senior Class in the spring of 1982.

She later attended Pepperdine University where she earned her Bachelor's Degree in Communication, and Masters Degree in Psychology in 2003. Her work experience includes working in the advertising and marketing department of the Los Angeles Lakers, Marketing and Communication Manager for the A.C. Green Foundation, Event Planner at Pepperdine University.

She was married to Robert Guy, though they eventually divorced. Their daughter, Taylor Elaine Guy, was born June 29, 2002. Crystal is a Bible School teacher, publicist, works with youth programs at the church, and volunteers at her daughter's school.

After leaving 74ᵗʰ Street School, B. was bussed to junior high and later to high school in Reseda, California, before eventually transferring to Palisades High. There, he passed the state high school proficiency test and graduated slightly ahead of his classmates. He enrolled at El Camino Community College and later transferred to Pepperdine.

His work experience has been diverse, beginning in high school working in the Photocopying Department at Pepperdine. He worked briefly at one Hollywood Studio, in restaurants as an assistant to the chef, lived briefly in Albuquerque, New Mexico, has traveled across the country with the National Youth Conferences, some on his own, and much like my brother, Herbert, B. would much rather drive than go near an airplane.

After Lori completed the 74ᵗʰ Street Elementary School, she was bussed to Paul Revere Middle School and later graduated to Pacific Palisades. In high school, she was a cheerleader.

After graduation, she enrolled at Pepperdine and graduated with a Bachelor of Science in 2000. Then she enrolled in the Graduate School of Education and Psychology and earned her Master's in Clinical Psychology, with an emphasis in Marriage and Family Therapy. She worked in several positions, finally ending up at Didi Hirsch Community Mental Health Center for Children in Inglewood, California.

Lori was very involved in local, state, and national Youth Conferences. She won the title of Miss National Youth Conference in 1997, in Arkansas. Later, she trained several other candidates who also won at the national level.

In 2001, she met Samuel Bailey at the Youth Conference held at the University of South Carolina. In December of 2002, they were married. They now reside in Grand Prairie, Texas. They have two lovely daughters, Madison Mozell, born October 25, 2006, and Reagan Ella, born October 28, 2009. Sam is the minister for the Cedarville Church of Christ.

Chapter 14

My Mother: Ollie's Passing

I KNEW SHE WAS GROWING OLDER, but she was still four years younger than my dad. She complained her health at times, but we always thought she would be alright. How many times had I thought, as we were leaving home, after coming from Illinois or Los Angeles, and seeing those two old folks sitting on the porch in the swing, "Will this be the last time?" Again and again we were blessed to return, but when we left, I always had that thought.

In July of 1976, the Figueroa Church of Christ had sent Mozell and me to Ethiopia. We left Crystal and Byron in Henderson, visiting our families, before going. After making the trip to the countryside and taking care of the business we were sent to do, we decided to return a few days early. Little did I know that when we came back to Tennessee to pick up our children, this would be the last time I would ever see Mom alive. I do not know the last thing I gave her, nor the last thing I said to her, but as we made that turn to drive to the main road, I remember that look of those two old people, my mother and my father, sitting on that old porch swing, in front of an old house, and that old feeling crept up on me again.

In August of 1976, my wife learned that she was expecting again. This time we could hardly believe that we were so happy. Then on a Saturday afternoon, I was concluding a Bible class in the home of Sister Collins, with a group of elderly ladies, when a call came. It was Mozell and she said, "Calvin, your mother just passed away." I was silent and the class knew that something was wrong. I told them that I just lost my mother. After thinking, *"What would she have me do?"* I announced I was going to finish that class, because I knew she would approve.

As I boarded the plane several days later for Memphis, I took a legal pad and began writing about my mother as soon as the plane was airborne. I wrote about how we went fishing, how she played ball with us after making the rag ball, and how she taught us games like the fox and the geese, which were so valuable in life as we faced problems in the world, and the sayings she gave us that guided us through life. As I neared Memphis, I began to realize that I really had not lost her because I still had everything she taught me.

She loved children. Mozell and I surmised that when the Lord took my mother, he would give us a daughter, and that proved to be the case. So whenever I hear a baby's cry, I was reminded of Mom; whenever I hear a good sermon from the Bible, she lives because she loved the Bible. Whenever I saw acts of kindness or love, I am reminded that she also lives in those acts because that was what she was about. The joy I felt in my heart gave me the strength to go through the funeral service in a fine way. Her spirit still sustains me, and I think of her often.

David Meek delivered the Eulogy and my brother-in-law Warren Blakney led the singing.

My Work at the Youth Conference

Beginning my work as a member on the Youth Conference board in 1958, and serving as Chairman for forty-six years thereafter, it was time to move on in 2002, at the Annual National Youth Conference when we met at the University of Ohio in Columbus. During my tenure, this conference of about 1,000 youth annually, from black Churches of Christ across the nation, visited almost every major city in the United States. These cities included, Detroit (home of the Conference), Chicago, Saint Louis, Boston, New York City, Nashville, Memphis, Knoxville, Chattanooga, New Orleans, Dallas, Houston, Tampa, Miami, San Francisco, Washington D.C., Champaign-Urbana, Flagstaff, Seattle, Denver, Los Angeles, Riverside, Abilene, and Oklahoma City, among so many more.

The men that I was blessed to work with included Orum Trone, Sr., Orum Trone, Jr., Dual Ghant, Carl Swanigan, Alvin Adkisson, Jesse Bishop, Ernest Wyrick and Clyde Muse. Each of these men had specific assignments and we respected each other. We had some differences, but we still worked together for the good of the youth.

The one woman who worked with us was Christine Trone, the wife of the Youth Conference founder Orum Trone, Sr. She was a marvelous companion and a tireless worker who had many helpful ideas. I appreciated her concern for details and her love for the youth.

The Work at the Figueroa Church of Christ Goes On

When I returned to Los Angeles in 1969, I agreed with Brother Hogan and the leaders not to neglect my work at the Church while working at Pepperdine. This was easier at first because the church, the Pepperdine campus, and my house were all within ten minutes drive of each other. Moving to the Malibu campus, thirty miles away, in 1976, made things a bit more difficult. I had to depend more on associate ministers and my secretaries Pamela Thompson at the church and Barbara Hood and Kim Williams at Pepperdine. We managed. During this time, Brother Hogan suffered a heart attack, which greatly limited his activity. He was still encouraging and did what he could.

We were able to continue our missionary work in Ethiopia, Nigeria, and the Bahamas. We also took the leading role in constructing a $500,000 church building and school structure in Addis Ababa, Ethiopia, on land that had been given to us by the government, through the efforts Eromo Kelbisow.

Domestic missionary efforts included starting a congregation in Star City, and Dumas, Arkansas. Later, additional elders and deacons to were added the Figueroa Church, and a number of new programs were developed. However, changing demographics and an aging congregation have, at times, impaired our growth. More recently with the addition of Darrell Holt, from Pontiac, Michigan, to our ministerial staff, things are appearing brighter. Starting with the Figueroa Garden Senior Citizen Home and the

R.N. Hogan Manor Family Housing Center, we hope to continue to evangelize the city of Los Angeles. Darrell Holt is training evangelistic teams well.

Chapter 15

My Dad Never Sat on the Loafer's Bench

AFTER MOM DIED, DAD LIVED FOR about ten more years, mainly cared for by Verble, who still lived less than a mile down the road.

It has been said that when you lose your dad, the wind blows directly on you. I never understood that better until the day my father died, on October 8, 1986, at his home in Selmer. There were so many things I still wanted to talk with him about. It seemed the older I became, the more wisdom he had to offer.

I remember that he took Mom's death very hard, and he said to Herbert and me, "She was a better woman than I was a man." We did our best to cheer him up for as long as he lived. Just as she had been for my mother, Verble became his major caregiver. She did her best to keep his house clean and presentable.

Most of my life, I thought of my dad as a tough man with some laid back moments but with Mom's passing, he became even more mellow. It seemed he had to go into town every day when we were young. He drove his pickup truck but after an accident he announced, "I have driven long enough."

Actually, he had begun shutting down before Mom passed. I chuckled when I went home and saw that their favorite TV show was "Captain Kangaroo." He had become a stay at home man, but continued to find something to do every day.

I believe that the highlight of his life was the trip to Decatur, Illinois and Des Moines in 1982. JoAnn, Herbert's wife, went from Des Moines to Tennessee, picked him up, and drove him back to Decatur to see family, then drove him to Des Moines for about a week. It occurred to me that he must have had a chuckle when, after all of those earlier years when he had to sit in the backseat when Nina Mae Latta was driving him to work, now he was riding with JoAnn, his daughter-in-law, who happened to be a white woman, and he was sitting in the front seat beside her. Herbert mentioned that he made the entire trip with the window down, in spite of the fact that Jo Ann had the air-conditioner on.

He had a great time in Decatur with his children and grandchildren, and he continued to enjoy himself in Des Moines, visiting the sights there. Herbert took him back to Decatur, and Major drove him back to Tennessee.

Once back in Tennessee, he concentrated on church attendance, gardening, and building things. With Verble's assistance, he was in church every Sunday. When things were not going well, or when he was bored, he would put his hoe on his shoulder and head across the road. He loved having a great garden and being able to give away turnip greens, string beans, and other vegetables. At the ripe old age of ninety-plus, he started building another house with no idea who would live in it or if it would ever be finished.

He told me, the last time I came home when he was still alive, "Cal, I can remember things that happened when I was a small child," then he paused and said, "I can't remember a thing from yesterday."

On October 8th, my sister Verble said Dad was smiling one moment, but when she turned away for a brief time, he was gone. At his funeral service, the eulogy was given by Rosie's husband, James. All the children were present, and for the first time, we all took a picture together as we mourned our loss.

When it came time for remarks, our retired high school principal, Professor Ledbetter, walked to the pulpit and closed his remarks by saying, "Mr. Henry Bowers was always at work, and no one could ever say he ever sat on the loafer's bench."

The First to Go

We did not know that Rosie was that sick. Though she'd had a serious condition two years before, she went on to make an amazing recovery. When I visited her in the middle of 2002, she seemed just fine with her usual smile and cheerfulness.

Later in the year, we received word that Rosie had to be on dialysis, but even then we had no idea it was life threatening. It seemed to me that she could make peace with the idea of dialysis and with the equipment. James, her husband, told me that somehow the needle came out and there was concern about the blood spillage.

A day or so later, while in route to the hospital, she began making a strange sound. James pulled the car over to the side of the road and soon she was gone. James, the loyal husband, was true to the end and he did all that could.

We were all deeply hurt over the first loss of the first of our siblings. Her life ended just as she lived it, with beauty and dignity. Her final services were held at the East Chester Church of Christ in Jackson, Tennessee with evangelist Gordon Newsome officiating. Eight years later, James C. Dixson passed away on January 10, 2010. His services were conducted at East Jackson Church of Christ on Chester Street on January 16, 2010 with evangelist Gordon Newsome again doing the eulogy.

Dorothy Passes Away

When I heard about Dorothy's terminal illness I was shocked. She was the healthy one, who walked several miles each day, had a number of pieces of exercise equipment to keep in shape, and watched her diet carefully. I thought she would be one of the last in family to go. But that was not to be the case.

During her married life she had done many things and filled many roles, besides being the mother of eight children. She had been an avid community worker, a cosmetics representative, a teacher's aide at an adult continuing education center, an assembly worker at the York division of Berg Warner, and the block club captain for the March of Dimes. She still found time for the Washington School PTA and was a member of the "Golden Girls" singing group of the Jasper Street Church of Christ.

As she grew weaker during the short period of her illness, I talked with her and her children often. When she could no longer speak, I talked with Howard. After I had prayer with all of the family, Howard said she was smiling. I thought this was the essence of the life she had lived.

She passed away on December 25, 2005, exactly two years, to the day, as Vernell. I was able to attend her final services at the Jasper Street Church of Christ on the December 30th. She was laid to rest in the Macon County Memorial Park.

I will always remember that Dorothy was the singular family member who gave me five dollars when I graduated from high school.

Losing the Center

When we lost Verble, we lost the heart of the family. Home was no longer home after Verble passed away; the center was gone. She had been there for Mom and Dad, and all of us. As I stated earlier, when we visited, we headed for Verble's before we stopped at the home of our parents.

She was the one who cooked the good meals and made us welcome in her home. She kept us up to date on the health status of our parents, as well as the status of the Forrest Hill Church of Christ, where she was dearly loved. Unlike Rosie, she had extended health problems. Among other things, her legs bothered her. She was in and out of the hospital many times. Jewell and Harold worked hard to meet her needs. I will forever be grateful to them for their help.

To never be a mother, she was like a mother to many of us. Danny and Joan Eubanks called her "mother" and she treated them like her children. It was unusual for a black church to have a white minister in that area, but Danny served as minister for the Forrest Hill Church of Christ for many years. They were also friends to most of our family. Mom and Dad loved Danny before they passed away.

When Verble passed on December 3, 2003, Danny was the logical one to conduct the funeral services on December 6th. I could not be present, but when I started writing this book, I asked Danny to write a statement to be included which I share, here, in its entirety:

> *Bro. Calvin,*
>
> *Jo Anne and I sat down and just started "rambling" about Sister Verble. I have no doubt written more than you can use in your book, but we thought you might enjoy any extra we would include. Go through and use what you want to and "cull" the rest.*
>
> *Our remembrance goes all the way back to the old Cypress Creek building where she and Bro. Flurice worshipped. That would have been in the mid 1960's. They were at that time working as custodians at the L & M Motel. As I remember she continued this for a while even after Bro. Flurice died. She told Jo Anne that motel work was "hard work". But Sister Verble didn't mind hard work. She always took care of her own house and yard as long as she could. I enjoyed helping her with small repair jobs about the house and working in her yard. She loved plants and flowers so much that you could hardly mow the yard for all the pots, trees, flowers, etc.*

About a year before she died, she was planting a fruit tree that she knew she would not live long enough to reap any fruit from, and when we asked her why she was planting it she said that she liked to leave «happy tracts» for those who would come after her.

She was always a very happy person who didn't complain about whatever her circumstances might be. She was very appreciative of even the smallest things done for her. We had what we considered a privilege to do many things for her. We wanted to because she was so grateful and loved us so much in return. She tried to repay me by always having some candy that she knew I liked—orange slices, and also some peanuts.

She had a far above average knowledge of the Bible. She always made very insightful comments in Bible class and would even tactfully correct any mistake made by the teacher or another student. She gave me several good sermon suggestions such as, «There is death in the pot».

Jo Anne has several of Sister Verble's choice comments written in the margin of her bible. Examples: Related to giving, "God doesn't accept tips from any of us." In regard to a Christian living an ungodly life she said, "You can detour through the Church straight into hell." "Sooner or later our true color will come out" meaning that what you really are will one day be obvious to all. She also said «when temptation rings the doorbell just don't go to the door." There are many, many more.

She was very content to live a very simple life, even heating her house with wood until the last few years of her life, when she finally got a gas heater. I have gone over a number of times (one time at 9:00 p.m.,) to relight the pilot light. She was so afraid of the gas heater and did not know how to relight it. She was always very apologetic about asking me to come, but I didn't mind at all.

We had the privilege of picking her up for worship, as we took our turn with other families. We enjoyed the conversations on the way to and from worship. We would occasionally go to Baskin Robbins for ice cream after worship and Jo Anne would tease her that even though they had 31 flavors she would always order vanilla.

We often told her we loved her and she would respond, "I know you do. I can feel it." Her wooden steps into the back porch had about rotted out, and we purchased and installed some new concrete steps. On the Sunday after we had installed them, as she got out of the car to go in she said with a grin, "Now just watch me walk up my new steps." We knew by that that she was proud and thankful for them.

We feel our lives have been truly blessed by being so closely associated with her, her parents, and several of her siblings—including the author! She was one of the most dedicated and delightful Christian

women we have ever known. We cherish her memory.
Thanks for the opportunity of sharing our memories
of her.

    Our love and respect to you Bro. Calvin, Danny,
and Jo Anne Eubanks

    P.S. You will probably find some misspelled
words. You know how to correct them.

Sarah the Servant

Although she was the oldest child, she was the third to pass away. Vernell passed on just twenty-one days after Verble, on Christmas day of 2003.

Her daughter, Gloria Jean, preceded her in death on June 22, 1989, and her husband, Kanoa, passed away May 23, 2000 in the Oak Manor Nursing Home of Decatur.

Sarah Vernell passed away in her sleep on Thursday, December 25, 2003 at the age of eighty-five. At her funeral services, Minister Mayo Towles spoke of the dark side and the bright side of death. The rest of her siblings realized they had lost a great treasure in her passing.

A next-door neighbor and friend, Marilyn Taylor, summed her passing in the tribute she made in a poem that she wrote:

    My Friend-Sarah Browning
    My friend, yes you are, whether near or far
    So near to my heart, a friend to all you are
    You took such pride in all your relationships
    Everyone was special, our ages didn't exist
    You spoke your mind, and we never had to wonder
    How you really felt, you didn't let us ponder.

How could anyone who suffered bravely at times like you
Continue to smile and bring joy, the whole year through
You had the sharpest wit, couldn't hide nothin' from you
You mentioned others having a lot of knowledge, but you had
it too!

You loved your daughter Gloria, your son Rolland and was
so proud of all your people
Everyone was special, from the street to the steeple
You will never leave me, because you're right here in
my heart
A true friend doesn't leave, so we will never part.

You made me laugh so much, on my face you kept a smile
Your charm kept others laughing, you made it all worthwhile
Your honesty and loyalty always embraced me
Your sincere concern for others continued to amaze me.

You love your animals, especially your dog, Rainbow, who
loved you too
I wouldn't think you'd want us to forget how much he meant
to you.
So rest dear friend, you're greatly loved, for God gave you
the best
On Christmas Day He embraced you and said, "Come home
my child and rest."

Losing Brother Bill

The last time I saw Bill was in March of 2005, when I attended a church leadership conference in Nashville, where he had lived for about thirty years. Along with Herbert, and our friend O.J. Dyson, we went to Bill and Bea's home on 24th Avenue North.

He was not as talkative as he had been in the past, but he smiled as we reminisced. Dyson took the last pictures of Bill, Herbert and me together. Although I had no idea that this was the last time I would see him or his wife, I could see that both were getting frail.

A short time after that visit, I learned through Jewell and her family that Bill had been placed in a local care center for seniors. When I got the phone number, I called and asked for him. We had a nice conversation, but I realized that his responses were not clear. Several times he asked me to repeat myself. Nevertheless, he seemed, like me, to enjoy that we were talking to each other.

After that, Herbert and I sent him some sweat clothes, fruit, and other items, in a care package. The people at the facility were very cordial and assisted us in whatever ways they could.

In mid-October of 2005, we received a phone call from Bill's daughter, Angelita, who had been trying to get my phone number. She informed me that Bill was seriously ill. She later got him on the phone for me, and I could hardly understand a word he said, but we kept the conversation going for as long as we could.

Soon thereafter, on Sunday, November 1st, Bill passed away. His services were held at the Terrell Broady Funeral Home, the following Thursday. The obituary mentioned his baptism in Selmer, his kids, Gregory and Angelita, his two decades of military service, his work in security at the Federal Reserve Bank in Nashville, and his personal work as an electrician. Jewell and Harold attended the services along with their family. Bill was laid to rest in the Greenwood Cemetery.

Chapter 16

Reflections on a Day

THIS WAS THE DAY HERBERT AND I had planned for some time. We wanted to visit the house of our sister Verble, who had passed in early December of 2003. I had this strange feeling that I had to go to Selmer, travel down the road to her house, go in, walk through the different rooms, and finally release her.

So many times I had traveled down this road to her house, and honked the horn, then saw her appear at the door, always smiling, and walking toward my car. About mid-distance, I could always hear her say, "It's so good to see you Calvin! How are you doing?" I would get out and as we would meet, she would give me a warm hug.

We would sit on the porch swing and talk about the things of life. After awhile she would dismiss herself, to check the food that she was preparing in the kitchen. No matter what time you arrived or what your schedule was, she expected you to eat. This provided for another level of conversation. The depth of the conversation grew the longer you stayed, wandering through her house, and her garden.

Finally, the visit would end, and she walked back to the car with you, still savoring every moment, still trying to cram in every second and all the information possible. As you pulled away, through the rearview mirror, you could see her standing there, watching the car drive out of sight.

I just couldn't give all of that up without my own special ceremony, so we had to make the visit that day. Herbert, who had the similar feelings, and Jewell and Harold who had been caring for Verble in her final days, joined Mozell and me for this closing of the curtain, one last visit with Verble.

I had been warned that the road to Verble's house had been blocked by the man who had bought my grandmother's old place. A new road had been built to move the logs from the pine trees on the farm. I saw the dirt, piled high, blocking the back road to her house, making it necessary for me to drive the Dodge Caravan up the steep hill of the front road. Just then, my resentment started to rise, because the way the dirt was placed sent a definite message: "Don't come through here." A slight rearrangement of the piled dirt would have easily made the road, which we had used for years, accessible.

Although the climb up the hill proved to be no challenge for the Caravan, the memory of my dad flashed through my mind, and at that moment I remembered how he had worked so hard to, "keep the white man at his distance." I also remembered that the same thing had happened to him, so many years earlier, when a white man had put up a fence on the road that led to our house, forcing us to make a new entrance road. He often warned, "Don't let the white man fence you in, or have your land."

The feelings I had as a child, when the road to our house was fenced off, all came back when I saw that dirt strategically placed which shouted, "Keep Out!" It was a feeling of psychological suffocation, a constricting feeling, like something is cutting off your air. It was a feeling that I definitely did not like. At that moment, Herbert, who must have either felt the same way or just sensed my feelings, broke the silence by saying, "Just a common courtesy would have left that road open." That helped some, but I still hurt and asked I myself, *"How far have we come and how far do we have to go?"*

As we approached the house we saw the weeds had grown up, and many of Verble's beautiful flowers were no longer blooming. I approached the front porch, to take a seat in the swing. Before I got there, Harold explained, "You can't go in the front door, we have to go around to the back." My steps became even more cautious walking through the grass. One step inside the back door I was met with the distinctive smell that said, "This is Verble's house." The only difference being that the house was stuffy and the smell was stronger.

As I slowly strolled from room to room, I was vividly reminded of the one who had occupied this house for so long. I remembered the food that was always on the table, which said I was always welcome. Her bedroom was stuffy, with only a few things having been removed. There were boxes filled and clothing, piled high.

Moving to the living room, I broke into a smile because the first thing I saw was owls; figurines and sculptures, dozens of them, and of all sizes. Here I remembered a time before Verble had passed, Mozell and I were visiting with her, and Mozell commented on Verble's collection of owls. Verble offered Mozell any she wanted, as a memento of the visit. She selected a set of three, of the smallest she could find, each about two inches high, which I still have today.

So on this day, as I moved through this room, reminiscing about my much beloved sister, I wondered out loud, "What was it that motivated Verble's love for the owls?" The eyes of her collection stared at me, but offered no answer, and by no stretch of my imagination could I figure it out.

I had a great feeling of satisfaction after that visit. It brought a sense of closure to the life of a sister that I loved so dearly. She had a great heart of love for so many, and opened her home as a haven for all the family members.

Mozell left us on September 8th of the same year, but I will always be glad that she was able to take the trip to Verble's house with me.

Changes

The year 2004 brought a number of significant changes in my life. After thirty-five years, I retired from Pepperdine University at Malibu, California. There were three retirement events. The first came from the administrative side of my work as University-wide Equal Opportunity Officer under Legal Counsel. Gary Hanson, Attorney over Legal Counsel, was my supervisor. He was a kind, understanding man who was helpful in my work. Together, we worked with challenging issues. This retirement ceremony was held on the fourth floor of the Thornton Center, near the University President's Office. My staff and a number of the administrators, including President Benton, were present. He presented me with two boxes of business cards and announced my new roles with the university as Professor Emeritus, and as Special Assistant to the President.

The second retirement event was in the Communication Division, where I had taught for so many years. The head of the division, Dr. Robert Chandler was present, along with the office staff and a number of the fellow professors. They presented me with a new printer. It was much needed and appreciated. My legacy at Pepperdine was represented in a mural in the new Communications building, showing me shaking hands with George Pepperdine, the school founder, in the 1960s.

The final event was a salute for a number of people who had worked for the university different numbers of years; some five, ten, twenty or thirty. Fortunately, I was one of the few that had worked thirty-five years and I was awarded a beautiful clock marking my years with the university. It was a wonderful evening, and I was very pleased to have Mozell and both of my daughters present.

As gratifying as that evening was, I was to reach an accompanying low within the next few months. On September 8, 2004, my wife of forty-seven years, Mozell, passed away after a brief illness. I was devastated because I had never experienced any pain like this.

As I left the Centinela Hospital after she passed, I listened to a song on a CD by Tiffany Malone, *Everything is going to be Alright When Jesus Comes.* In my tears, it gave me strength. It was through the love and care of my family members, church family, neighbors, and those who sent their love from all over the country that I was able to go on with my life.

Along with her sister, Juanita Trice of Los Angeles, we carried her body back to Henderson, Tennessee, where we had a service at the Oak Grove congregation, where she had grown up, then brought her back to the Figueroa Church of Christ in Los Angeles for the final service. Returning with us to Los Angeles were her sisters

Wilma Harville, Christine Trice, Patricia Blakney and her husband Warren, and Brenda DePriest and her husband Richard. The year 2004 ended on a sad note for me. Everything reminded me of her, and I could not deny the pain I was experiencing.

A New Direction

During my period of healing, Brother David Jones asked me to be the banquet speaker at the 2005 Annual Lectureship held in Nashville, Tennessee. From the beginning, I wanted to go. My brother Herbert, living in Des Moines, agreed to meet me in Nashville. Crystal, and my granddaughter, Taylor, and O.J. Dyson traveled with me. On the night of the banquet, there were over 2,000 people in the audience. As I spoke, I mentioned the loss of my wife and how difficult it was for me to grasp scriptures, such as, "In everything give thanks; for this is the will of God in Christ Jesus concerning you," from I Thessalonians 5:18, and "And we know that all things work together for good to them that love God, to them who are called according to His purpose," Romans 8:28. I went on to say my understanding was improving because I began to realize that Mozell loved God too, and He knew what was best.

In that audience, there was a Christian woman from Clinton, Oklahoma who also loved God. After the service she came to the front, to exchange a plaque, which had been given to her earlier by mistake, and she almost bumped into me.

We introduced ourselves. She extended her sympathy over the loss of my wife and as she was about to go, I said, "Call us sometime." She did and we began talking, and on August 19, 2006, Barbara Hayes became Mrs. Calvin Bowers. We both feel blessed that God allowed us to get together. We have continued our life together at the Figueroa Church of Christ.

Since that time I have continued my ministry, preaching, conducting teacher training and other types of workshops, writing, including editing a quarterly for 21st Century Christian Publications and developing a group called Fellow Workers for Christ, with the goal of training 1,000 preachers, 1,000 Bible School teachers, and 1,000 leaders. In June of 2010, Darrell Holt was added to the staff as a qualified and capable minister. This allows even more time for me to work on special efforts to glorify the Lord.

Currently, I am upgrading my technological skills to have the best methods of serving, utilizing, and dispersing information.

Conclusion

A Glance Backward for a Look Forward

WHEN I BEGAN WRITING THIS BOOK, I felt an urgency to write, because of the hard times my mother, and many like her, had, who were all determined to give their children a better life. In spite of their great difficulties, they still had time to laugh, enjoy their families, and live strong in the Church.

I began as a guide to you on this journey, but in many ways I was the explorer. I was discovering myself. In the questionnaires I sent to my siblings, the photos we almost had to literally dig up, the conversations with my nieces and nephews, and connecting all of this with my own children and grandchildren, I was reminded of one of the reasons I wanted to honor my mother in the title of this book.

I've mentioned that sense of security her quilts provided, my fascination with the process of making them, and their warmth. And as I've written this I've seen where those quilts, their security,

220

warmth, and construction was a metaphor for the family Ollie and Henry have created.

My purpose has expanded, as their family has expanded, for not only must I write looking back, but I must write, and look around, and look ahead and, most of all look up. As Ollie Mae Ella made quilts from many diverse pieces and sewed them into a whole, her family has had that same diversity. As Henry Harrison made a framework for her quilting, with the same care for strength and stability as he put into the houses he built, he created a framework for our family.

We're all Ollie's kids. It was the struggles and the survival of women like her, from before her time and since her time that got us all here today. It will be through the same efforts of us today that our children, grandchildren, and great-grandchildren will build their own families. But we must build the frame and provide the same warming quilt.

So, I write looking around with the faith that my three children will always remember what their mother, Mozell, and I tried to teach them to do their very best to follow those guidelines and pass them on to their children.

I write for my three little granddaughters, Taylor Elaine, Madison Mozell, and Reagan Ella, that they will read what I write, and connect themselves with the legacy of their great-grandparents, Ollie and Henry, and what they did, when they faced difficult times in life.

But as I reflect, I write for all those under the quilt: my nieces and nephews Rolland, Gregory, Angelita, Brenda, Glynis, Janis, Kenny, Terry, David, Howard, Ollie Inez, Judy, Charles, JoAnne, Dorothy Nell, Herbert Jr., Bonita, Ricky, Sylvia, Joe, and Chris.

My prayer is that each of them remembers where they came from, the principles of life and love their grandparents instilled in their parents and to pass it on to their children and grandchildren. And of course, I cannot forget my nephews and nieces who are no longer with us. Gloria Jean, Richard, Joseph and Marsha will always be in our hearts as a part of a family journeying under the beautiful quilt made by Ollie and Henry Bowers.

My goal remains the same: to be a Christian man and my determination is as the Bible says, "Yea, I think it meet, as long as I am in this tabernacle, to stir you up by putting you in remembrance;" II Peter 1:13, 14.

Under Grandmother's Quilt

By Calvin H. Bowers

Under the quilt that grandmother made,
It gives some warmth,
It gives others shade.

It makes us all feel so near,
It gives some strength to face each fear.

Some of us are close,
And others are far,
But to her, each child was a superstar!